The Restless Missionary

by Virgil Robinson

Pencil Drawings by Fred Collins

TEACH Services, Inc.
PUBLISHING
www.TEACHServices.com • (800) 367-1844

Copyright © 2013 Virgil Robinson and TEACH Services, Inc.
ISBN-13: 978-1-4796-0087-8 (Paperback)
ISBN-13: 978-1-4796-0088-5 (ePub)
ISBN-13: 978-1-4796-0089-2 (Kindle/Mobi)

Library of Congress Control Number: 2012955215

Published by

TEACH Services, Inc.
P U B L I S H I N G
www.TEACHServices.com • (800) 367-1844

Contents

With a sense of mission like that of Paul and the ardor of John the Baptist, Joseph Wolff penetrated the Moslem world, heralding the second advent of Jesus.

1
The Wandering Child

IT WAS a quiet Sabbath afternoon in the little town of Halle, Germany. A group of rabbis had gathered at the home of David Wolff. As so often happened, their thoughts turned to the great events that had occurred during the long history of the Jews since Moses humbled Pharaoh's pride.

They spoke of the glories of their nation during the reigns of David and Solomon. They rubbed their hands together in satisfaction over the beauteous Esther who turned the tables on the proud and wicked Haman.

In one corner of the room, listening intently, sat little Wolff, the eight-year-old son of Rabbi David. He was handsome in his black velvet suit, his elbows resting on his knees, and his chin in his hands. As he gazed at those gray-bearded rabbis, he was sure they were the wisest men on earth.

Then the rabbis spoke of the long, dark ages when Jews had been relentlessly persecuted throughout Europe. Thousands and thousands had been killed. There was anger in their voices as they spoke of those terrible times. Then from the sad record of the past they turned to speak of the glories of the coming kingdom, when Messiah should appear and the Jews would rule the world. *Then* the Gentiles would know what submission meant!

Little Wolff became quite excited, although he couldn't understand all he had heard. The next morning he wandered down the street to talk with his good friend Spiess, the barber-surgeon. Sitting on a high stool, his little legs dangling, Wolff repeated what he thought he had heard.

"Do you know, sir," he said, "that when Messiah comes, He will kill the great fish Leviathan that eats ten million of every kind of fish every day and that is as large as the whole world and He will also kill the large ox that feeds every day on three thousand mountains, and the Jews will eat of that fish and of that ox when Messiah comes!" Little Wolff's eyes flashed and grew large with the wonder of it all.

Turning toward Wolff, the old man spoke very softly, very kindly.

"Wolff, I will tell you who the Messiah was. He was Jesus of Nazareth, the Son of God Your fathers crucified Him, as they did the prophets of old. Go home and read the fifty-third chapter of Isaiah."

Wolff, young as he was, went home and read that chapter, and when he finished his heart was troubled. He went to his father with his Hebrew Bible.

"Father." Wolff looked into the well-beloved face. "Who is the prophet speaking about here?"

The father looked at the passage to which his son pointed and an expression of great sadness crossed his face. He knew very well that a Christian must have told his son to read that passage and ask that question. He turned and walked away, speechless. Little Wolff dared not repeat his question. But that night, when his parents thought he was sleeping, he heard them talking in the next room. "I know not what will become of our son," the father said.

"I fear he will not long remain a Jew. He is continually walking about asking questions and thinking. It is not natural." Then Wolff heard his mother weeping.

Little Wolff attended a Protestant school in Halle for a time, and there he heard more about Jesus. One day he plucked up courage to speak again to his father.

"Who was this Jesus the Christians talk about?"

"He was a Jew of the greatest talent," the man answered sadly. "But because He said He was the Messiah, the Jews put Him to death."

Little Wolff thought about that for a long time. On another day came another question.

"Why is Jerusalem destroyed, and why are we in captivity?" "Alas," replied his father, "it is because our fathers murdered the prophets."

Little Wolff said nothing more, but he went on thinking.

One day a rabbi asked the eleven-year-old boy what he wanted to be.

"I should like to be a doctor, or perhaps a great preacher. I should even like to be the pope of Rome."

Astonished, the rabbi hurried to the father and mother. "Woe, woe, woe!" he exclaimed. "Your son will not remain a Jew." Then he repeated what the little boy had said.

When Wolff became a little older he decided to see the world. For a beginning he paid a visit to his rich Uncle Asshur, whose home was in a nearby town. The old man was happy to see his nephew, but he warned the boy not to mingle with Christians unnecessarily. Perhaps he had heard about the questions the boy had asked when he was younger.

"If you forsake the religion of your fathers," the uncle warned, "I will not leave you any of my money."

"Oh, that's all right," Wolff replied. "Just leave it to my brother; he needs it much more than I do."

From there he journeyed to Bamberg and stayed for a time with his cousin, Moses Cohen. There he read the New Testament for the first time. He came to know much more about Jesus, and he was especially fascinated with the story of Saul, who became Paul. "That's what I am going to be," he exclaimed, "a great missionary, and travel to far countries!"

His cousin only laughed at such a prophecy. But his cousin's wife became furious, hurled a poker at Wolff, and turned him out of the house.

Wolff was penniless and friendless. As he wandered along the road, a chill wind began to blow down from the mountains. The sun set, and Wolff began to wonder where he could sleep. A shepherd passed, returning with his sheep from a day in the hills. "What are you doing out here all alone?" he asked the boy.

"I don't know where I can sleep tonight. I have no money for the inn."

"Come home with me," the kind shepherd invited, and led the youthful wanderer to his hut. Here Wolff shared a frugal meal with the shepherd and his family.

"Tell us about yourself," the host requested.

When he had listened attentively to Wolff's story, the man said, "Then you are not a Catholic?"

"No," replied Wolff, fearing that perhaps he might again be turned out. "We are a Jewish family." But he was allowed to stay.

Before retiring, the shepherd and his wife knelt to pray. The man took out a string of beads, known as a rosary. He said: "Let us recite five Ave Marias and one Paternoster [Lord's Prayer] for the soul of this poor Jew, that the Lord may guide him into His fold."

The next morning the kind shepherd gave Wolff some breakfast. "Friend," he said, as the lad was leaving, "you are in distress. Allow me to share with you what I have. Here are two florins. They will carry you well to Frankfurt."

As Wolff went on his way he knew he could never forget the kindness of that Christian shepherd.

Within a month he returned to Halle, only to find that his father had died and that he was now homeless. He decided to go to Prague and become a Catholic. Before leaving Halle, he went to the Christian school he had attended, and from his teachers he obtained letters of introduction. With these he journeyed hundreds of miles eastward to the famous city of Prague.

As soon as he arrived in the city he went to one of the famous monasteries and requested the abbot to baptize him into the Christian faith. The man refused.

"How do I know this is not just a trick?" he asked. "You have quarreled with your father. You told him that you would become a Christian just to spite him."

Wolff went to another priest and repeated his request for baptism.

"Listen," said the priest, "I can see that you are very clever. If you remain with the Jews, you can become famous. But if you become a Christian, nobody will ever hear of you, for there are thousands of clever Christians. Take my advice and stay with the Jews."

Greatly discouraged, Wolff made his way to another large Catholic city, Vienna.

Before you finish reading the life of Wolff you will discover an interesting fact about him. He never liked to remain in one place very long, and moved constantly from place to place. So, after visiting Vienna for a few weeks, he decided to pass on to Munich. On his way he stopped at another monastery.

Wolff had discovered that the monks in these places would usually treat a stranger with hospitality, giving him supper and a place to sleep. But he also found that the monks were lazy.

Knowing that he was a Jew who desired to become a Christian, the cook at the monastery thought she would test him. She offered him a piece of pork, a food most Jews will not eat. Wolff consented to eat it. But when she entered the room with the meat, she spoke some insulting words about Moses. Flaming with anger, Wolff leaped from his chair, slapped her face, and rushed out of the monastery. All his life he would have to battle with a fiery temper.

At Munich he decided to attend a famous Protestant university.

Perhaps he might become a Protestant Christian rather than a Catholic. Wolff was accepted as a student, but he was told that in addition to his studies he must acquire two accomplishments— one was dancing and the other was painting.

At this school he struggled to master both skills, but with little success. Finally a man in the town promised to do his drawing if Wolff would teach him Hebrew. All went well until Wolff boasted in school of how he was deceiving his teachers.

When the schoolmaster heard of this he became very angry. He had Wolff whipped and placed in a dungeon for twenty-four hours on a diet of bread and water. In spite of this Wolff remained in Munich for six months, then decided to go to a town called Weimar.

On the way he stayed at another monastery college in Gunter. Here he became friendly with a Catholic named Biederman. One night he decided to tell his friend a little about himself.

"Do you know who I really am?" he asked.

Biederman gazed at him in surprise.

13

He had Wolff whipped and placed in a dungeon for
twenty-four hours on a diet of bread and water.

"Well, I have had doubts about your Christianity ever since you came. When we stand for prayer, you sit, and when we kneel, you stand. Who are you?"

"I am a Jew who wants to become a Christian." Leaping out of bed, Biederman raised a great shout. "Help! Help!" he screamed.

"Whatever is the matter?" asked the abbot, rushing in. "Have you seen the devil?"

"Worse than that," replied Biederman. "This man Wolff is a Jew..."

Wolff then had to explain to the angry abbot that he had been born a Jew but was really a Christian at heart, after which the men calmed down and allowed him to stay.

Every morning before breakfast all the monks bowed in unison to a small image placed in a niche in the wall. During this ceremony Wolff would turn and gaze out the window. The students were horrified, and demanded that he either bow to the image or leave. Wolff left and went to Prague.

The abbot there received the seventeen-year-old youth kindly. After answering many questions, he was baptized into the Catholic Church. He was given the name of Joseph, and from then on he was called Joseph Wolff.

"What are your plans?" the abbot asked him.

"I want to be a missionary to Asia," Wolff replied.

"Then go to Rome," the abbot replied. "That is where missionaries are trained."

"That is just what I plan to do," Wolff said. Shortly after, he left for Vienna en route to Rome.

2
On the Road

WHEN he arrived in Vienna, Joseph Wolff met some sincere people who became his friends. They were Catholics, and they were deeply interested in the story of how he had changed from Judaism to Catholicism.

Wolff taught Hebrew for a while to support himself. But his restless spirit urged him on, in spite of the new friends he had made. He decided to visit the well-known Count Stalburg in Westphalia.

Joseph carried with him a letter of introduction from the kindly bishop of Vienna. Nearing the town, he asked a stranger where the count lived, and was directed to a castle standing on a high hill. Walking up the long tree-lined avenue, his courage almost failed him. "No," he said to himself; "I will go on. I am as good as anyone else. If the count doesn't want to see me, he can command me to go."

At the castle a haughty servant announced Wolff's presence to the count. The great man entered the hall. Wolff handed him the letter from the bishop. After scanning it, the count began to ask Joseph all about himself. For a long while they talked together.

Joseph opened his bag and took out some sheets of paper.

"What have you there?" asked the count.

"A sermon that I composed."

"Read me some of it."

Joseph obeyed. While he was doing this the door opened. Into the room came the count's beautiful wife with her children. Wolff could hardly believe his eyes as the family followed eleven sons and seven daughters!

"These are my children," the count said. "You can teach them much. Stay here and make your home with us."

So for several months Joseph stayed with the kind family. One morning while the group were at breakfast a servant handed a sealed paper to the count. Hastily he opened it and read the contents. His face turned pale, his hands began to tremble, and he rose angrily from the table.

"What is it, my dear?" the countess asked fearfully. "Napoleon has left the island of Elba and has returned to France. He is marching on Paris. This means more fighting!" He looked around the table at his stalwart sons.

"Some of you will have to go. This is Napoleon's last attempt. God will cast him down."

A few days later Wolff watched three of the young men ride off to the war. It was a heartbreaking scene. The countess clung to her boys, weeping.

"It breaks my heart to part from you," she sobbed, "but as Christians, you must go."

Soon afterward, while Wolff was still there, the sad news came that the two oldest sons had been killed in the Battle of Waterloo.

After a few more weeks Joseph continued the journey that was to take him to Rome. On the way he stopped at a Protestant school. While there he spoke in defense of the Catholic Church.

"You don't know the Catholic Church," the students said to him. "Go to Rome. You will soon discover that if you talk there as you talk here, you will be put into prison."

"I don't believe it," Wolff replied, "but I shall find out."

First, however, Wolff decided he must learn what Protestants really believe. So he went to Tübingen. There he found that he must pay for all his meals. If he had been a Protestant he would have been fed free. Nearly penniless, Joseph wrote immediately to the king of Prussia, stating who he was and mentioning his friendship with Count Stalburg and asking for free board at the school. Surprisingly enough, the king replied that Wolff should not be required to pay.

To Joseph's astonishment and sorrow he found that many of the teachers in that school did not believe the Bible. This discovery turned his footsteps unhesitatingly toward Rome. He had heard of a famous school there called the Missionary College of Propaganda. At that place he would prepare to go out as a missionary to heathen lands.

Ever journeying southward, he traveled over many roads through many towns to Switzerland, walking by day and resting overnight with friendly monks in monasteries located in the various towns.

He found that Basel, Switzerland, was a strong Protestant city. Learned men there warned him against going to Rome.

"You will have trouble unless you admit that the pope is in fallible," they said. "That means making him equal with God."

"That I will never believe!" Wolff declared emphatically.

"In Rome you cannot be a good Catholic unless you do believe it," they replied.

"That remains to be seen," Wolff said, unconvinced.

At one monastery he took out his Hebrew Bible and began to read it silently, as was his custom. The abbot came and took it out of his hands.

"What is this you have?" he asked.

"It is my Hebrew Bible."

The abbot glanced through it, then put it into his own pocket. Reaching out his hand, Wolff requested the Book back.

"You cannot have it again," the abbot said firmly. "I am going to burn it."

"Why should you do that?" asked the bewildered Wolff.

"Because it was printed in Holland, which is a heretic country. Therefore this is a heretic Bible and dangerous for you to possess."

So Wolff had to journey on without his Bible. But at the very next town he stopped and purchased another Bible. That night at the next monastery the same thing happened. The abbot took the new Bible from him.

"But what is the matter with this Bible?" Wolff was exasperated.

"Look here." The abbot turned to the front page. "See, it was printed in Leipzig, a Protestant city. This is a heretic Bible, and you must not have it."

Making no outward protest, Wolff watched carefully and saw where the abbot put his precious Book. During the night he arose, found his Bible, tucked it into the bottom of his knapsack, and in the morning went on his way.

All through Switzerland, Wolff was repeatedly warned, "Don't go to Rome. You will disappear and nobody will ever see you again."

"That remains to be seen," was Wolff's constant reply to these warnings, and he trudged on along the country road. It began to rain. Not only what he was wearing but everything in his knapsack was soaked. Seeing a convent near the road, he knocked on the door, hoping to find shelter for the night.

The mother superior was startled to see this dripping stranger. When he explained who he was and where he was going, she invited him in. Soon he was sitting by a fire in the parlor, telling a group of nuns the story of how he had been a Jew but was now a Christian.

The nuns were fascinated by his many adventures. Food was set before him. Then the mother superior wrote a letter to the magistrate of a nearby village. Wolff went there and was given dry clothing to wear while his own clothes dried before the fire. The kindhearted man gave him money so he could travel by stage coach to the next city, Turin.

In those days Turin was the capital of a small Italian kingdom. The German ambassador there was also kind to Wolff, giving him money so he might journey by stagecoach all the way to the large city of Genoa.

"When you reach Genoa, Wolff, take a ship down to Ostia," the ambassador said. "This is much cheaper than going by stage coach all the way. At Ostia you will be only a few miles from Rome."

So when Joseph reached Genoa he went to the water front to find a ship going to Ostia. He found one, but alas, the wind was contrary. Many days passed as the ship remained at anchor, waiting for the wind to change. Three long weeks passed. Wolff had used up nearly all of his money for food, and not enough remained to get him to Ostia. So when the wind finally changed and the ship set sail, he could only pay his fare to the city of Leghorn.

With only two florins in his pocket and his knapsack on his back, he decided to walk to Rome, one hundred forty-five miles away. He found the sun hot and the road dusty. Feeling faint from the heat, he flung himself down under a tree and wondered what he should do.

He looked this way and that. Not a house nor a person could he see. The sky was empty, the road was empty, and his stomach was empty.

Right there by the side of the road Wolff knelt down and prayed. Then he sat and waited for the help he had asked God to send. Half an hour later a small cloud of dust appeared far down the valley, grew larger, and soon a stagecoach was stopping for him.

"How much must I pay to go to Pisa?" Wolff asked.

"Two florins," the driver replied.

Wolff pulled out his last two florins, gave them to the driver, and climbed aboard. On the coach he met a naval officer traveling to Rome. The two were soon enjoying a good visit.

"You say you are going to Rome?" the officer asked.

"That's right."

"Well, then, why are you getting off at Pisa?" "That is as far as my money will take me." "Can you find more money in Pisa?"

"I don't know a soul there."

"Do you have friends in Rome?"

"Not yet, but I hope to have many soon after I get there." Suddenly an idea came to Wolff.

"Perhaps you will lend me the money I need in order to ride all the way to Rome. You can keep my knapsack as security."

A smile crossed the officer's face.

"I will be happy to lend you the money, but please keep your knapsack. You look honest, and I am sure I can trust you." So it was settled, and the officer told Wolff where he lived in Rome. On the fourth day they crossed the boundary into the papal state ruled by the pope. Wolff made the sign of the cross. When he saw a large sign over the road he rejoiced to read upon it the one Latin word *pax*, meaning "peace." But when a little farther on he saw a group of prisoners in chains working on the road, he wondered whether he would truly find that all was peace in the kingdom of the pope.

The sun was setting as the coach neared the city's boundaries. Eager for his first view of the place he had so long waited to be hold, Wolff stuck 1-Js head out of the window and gazed at the city on the seven hills. There stood Rome, the Eternal City, his destination. There stood the great dome of St. Peter's Cathedral. There he would see the pope. In his heart he wondered how this mighty city would influence his future.

3
A Student in Rome

ON HIS first morning in Rome, Joseph Wolff went to see Cardinal Litta.

"I want to be a missionary like Francis Xavier," he declared. "Then you should enter the College of Propaganda, but unfortunately it is closed for repairs and will not reopen for a year or more. There is a school operated by the pope, but it is open only to Italians. The pope himself is the only one who could get you in there."

"Then I must see the pope," Wolff said.

The cardinal smiled. "Not so fast, my young friend, not so fast. You will see the pope some time; I cannot say when. Where are you staying?"

Wolff told him the name of the monastery where he was lodging.

"Very well, I shall notify you when the pope is able to see you," and with this the cardinal dismissed him.

For a month Joseph waited. He wandered all over Rome, looking with amazement at its famous buildings and ruins. The monks showed him many wonderful sights, including the places where they thought Peter had been crucified and Paul beheaded.

One day there was a celebration in the plaza in front of St. Peter's Cathedral. Wolff was present, along with thousands of other onlookers. For the first time he saw the pope, but he could not speak to him. Joseph beheld an old, tired-looking man. Pope Pius VII had endured harsh treatment at the hands of Napoleon Bonaparte.

But at last the great day arrived. Word came that Monsignor Testa, the papal secretary, would take him in to see the pope the next morning. That was August 9, 1816. Wolff was then twenty years old.

The pope had already heard of him and seemed pleased to meet him.

"He received me," wrote Wolff later, "not as a king receives one of his subjects, but as a father would welcome his son."

Knowing the customs of Rome, Wolff was prepared to bow and kiss the pope's foot, but Pius VII would not allow this. Instead, he held out his hand, and Wolff reverently kissed that. Then the pope asked Wolff to read to him from a Hebrew Bible, and was delighted to see how easily he could do so.

"You are my son," he said. "The College of Propaganda is not yet ready to reopen, but I have arranged for you to enter my own seminary."

Wolff patted Pius on the shoulder.

"I love Your Holiness," he said, and fell on his knees. "Give me your blessing." Kneeling there, Wolff listened while the pope blessed him in Latin.

In the seminary Wolff found that he was the only foreigner among a large number of Italian students. At first he got along very well. He still felt humbled by the honor of being admitted. He was proud of his purple gown and three-cornered hat. He was proud of associating with students who were monks preparing to go out as missionaries. Sometimes he found it hard to adjust, as when he had to obey the rule of silence, which at times was en forced for two long days and nights. This was very hard on a young man who liked to talk more than he liked to eat or sleep.

Every now and then returning missionaries would visit the seminary and tell of all their deeds in distant lands. This made Wolff all the more eager to be on his way.

Every morning the students listened to long lectures. You would think them very dry and uninteresting. So did Wolff at times, and he would then take out his Hebrew Bible and read as the lecturer droned on. The other students were shocked.

One lecturer was discussing an early church writer, St. Augustine. He stated that if the pope did not agree with St. Augustine, then they must accept the verdict of the pope, not that of St. Augustine. Wolff, up near the front of the class, suddenly stood up.

In a loud voice he asked, "Do you believe that the pope is infallible and never makes any mistakes?"

"Yes," the irritated lecturer replied.

"Well," replied Wolff, "I do not."

The statement created an uproar. Looking sternly at Wolff, the lecturer remarked, "Bad and impious people seldom believe in the infallibility of

In a loud voice Wolff asked, "Do you believe that the pope is
infallible and never makes any mistakes?"

the pope. If you want to remain here, you had better drive away such impious thoughts."

As soon as the lecture was over, Wolff rushed to his friend, Cardinal Litta, to tell him about it.

"You don't have to believe everything you hear, Wolff," the cardinal said, trying to calm the youth, "but keep it to yourself. It was very bad form to interrupt as you did. After all, you are eating the food of the seminary. Therefore, you must treat the teachers with respect."

One lecturer taught church history. As the story came nearer and nearer to the time of Luther, Wolff could hardly wait. He wanted to hear what would be said about the great German Reformer. Just when it seemed that the lecturer would have to discuss Luther the next day, he went back to the beginning for a review.

"Why?" Wolff asked.

"It is our custom," the man replied. Wolff was disgusted. One day while they were eating, Wolff's tongue got him into trouble again. A student turned to him and asked, "Wolff, how could you dare to pat the pope's shoulder? Are you not aware that the pope is God?"

Red with anger, Wolff turned to his questioner, shouting, "How dare you say such a thing? The pope is dust of the earth! If he were God I could not have touched him!"

A terrible uproar arose in the dining room. Shouts of "Heretic! Heretic!" rang through the hall. Professors and students leaped to their feet, shouting, "Wolff, Wolff, whatever are you saying?"

Joseph turned to his teacher.

"This fellow says that the pope is God, and I say he is dust of the earth. Who is right?"

"He is God on earth," came back the answer.

"I may call him God in a large sense," stated another.

"Well, I refuse to call him God in either a large or a small sense. He is dust of the earth."

Wolff's fellow students, especially his close friends, urged him to keep quiet. But they could no more keep Wolff quiet than they could prevent the sun from shining.

One day a group of students surrounded him.

"Wolff, what are you going to become?" they questioned.

"I am going to be the pope someday, and I shall take the name of Hildebrand I."

Bursting into uproarious laughter, the students touched their foreheads. Now they were positive that Wolff was crazy. But Joseph was very sincere in all his beliefs. He could not pretend that he believed a thing when he did not.

About this time the College of Propaganda reopened, and Wolff was transferred to it. But it was now evident to his superiors that Wolff would never make a dependable Catholic missionary. Almost weekly there were reports of more dashes between Wolff and his fellow students, or of even more serious clashes with his teachers.

One day a class was discussing Jansen, a noted French leader. "If the church had burned him, she would have done well," the professor said.

Said Wolff with great indignation, "The church has no right to bum."

"How do you prove that?"

"The commandment says, 'Thou shalt not kill.'"

"The shepherd has a right to kill a wolf that enters the sheepfold."

"A man is not a wolf."

"Seventeen popes have burned heretics."

"Seventeen popes have done wrong," Wolff boldly declared. Students and professors alike were stunned. For a few moments they were completely speechless. Wolff looked around the table to see whether there might be at least one courageous soul who would stand with him. As his eye swung past the partly open door, he saw standing behind it a tall, distinguished-looking gentleman. This man was moving his finger at Wolff, indicating that he wished to speak with him. Excusing himself, Wolff left the silent lecture hall.

The man was Henry Drummond, a wealthy English banker in Rome on business.

"Wolff," he asked, "what are you doing here? You can't talk like that around this city. Come with me to England."

Wolff shook his head. "No, I shall not stir from Rome until I am turned out."

Shrugging his shoulders, Mr. Drummond said, "That shouldn't take long if you go on as I heard you just now."

Drummond then went on his way, but he did not forget the young man who was in such a dangerous position.

Again Wolff went to Cardinal Litta. The cardinal was displeased with what he had heard about the discussion in the lecture hall. "Wolff, you must learn to obey in silence," he said, and that was all.

Warnings began to come to Wolff. "You are in danger. Be careful of what you write." He discovered that his letters were being censored. In them he had discussed freely his true feelings about the subjects discussed in college.

He received a letter from Drummond, now in England. "Wolff," it said, "come out of Babylon." But Wolff still wanted to go the other way. He replied, "I shall go to the East and preach the gospel to the Jews."

Some of his letters fell into the hands of the officers of the Inquisition. These men were appointed to see that no heretics could live and work in Rome. They fully realized that Wolff would never make a faithful Roman Catholic.

After some weeks Wolff was moved from his room at the college to a small room near the Inquisition offices. No one was allowed to visit him. The place was searched, and all his writings were inspected. His fellow students were questioned about any statements he made.

Soon Joseph received another, more severe, shock. A tailor came in quietly, measured him from head to foot, wrote down his measurements, and without uttering a word, departed. He was followed by a shoemaker who measured his feet. Last of all, a hatter came and measured his head. Why are they doing this? poor Wolff wondered. Are they getting ready to bury me?

At last his friend, Cardinal Litta, came. He reproached Wolff for the many disturbances he had caused.

"We have been very patient, Wolff," he said, "but you will never be of any use to us until you change your thinking. We are sending you to the archbishop in Vienna. Here is a letter to the bishop of Bologna, where you will be stopping on the way."

The next evening a man led Wolff into another room. There lay a new suit of clothes, a new pair of shoes, and a new hat. Now he understood why they had taken his measurements.

No one was allowed to tell him good-by. A coach drew up at the door. With an officer of the Inquisition, Wolff embarked. The curtains were drawn, and the coach rattled off into the night. Feeling very uneasy, Wolff wondered whether he was about to meet his end in some secret prison, a victim of the Inquisition.

4
Turned Around

A S THE coach rattled on through the night, Wolff wondered about the man who was guarding him, whose dim outline he could see on the opposite seat. He wondered, too, about the letter in his pocket. Every time his fingers touched it, he longed for solitude and light so that he could scan the message intended for the eyes of the bishop of Bologna. Did it contain instructions that would result in his imprisonment? Or even worse—would he be executed? His memory brought back some of the warnings Protestants in Switzerland had whispered in his ear. Perhaps they had been right.

When the coach stopped at an inn, the two weary travelers got out. The guard saw Wolff put away safely in a room. Wolff heard the key turn and realized that he was a prisoner for the remainder of the night. But at least he could now satisfy his curiosity.

By the light of a candle on a small table near his cot, he pulled out the letter and carefully opened it. To his surprise and pleasure, it contained nothing dangerous, but only friendly greetings and a request that the bishop of Bologna should take good care of Wolff.

Wolff now felt ashamed for having opened the letter. Then another thought came to him. What about the letter the guard carried in *his* pocket? Perhaps that one carried the dangerous instructions. Poor Wolff obtained but little sleep during the few hours he spent at the inn.

Next morning the men were on their way again. The warmth of the morning sun and the motion of the coach gradually lulled the guard to sleep, his coat hanging over his arm. Wolff eyed the letter sticking out of its pocket. Slowly, cautiously he reached out, trying to grasp it without waking the guard But the moment his fingers touched the coat, the guard opened his eyes. Gently he pushed Wolff's hand away.

"It's no use, Wolff. I am not asleep. Furthermore, I have no intention of going to sleep." He smiled grimly.

All was silence as the coach jogged through the pleasant Italian countryside. Wolff was filled with self-reproach. Why had he been so imprudent at Rome and made so many enemies? Why had he not kept his opinions to himself? Why had he continuously been the storm center of controversy? Perhaps he would be killed in some secret place. He could only pray silently for deliverance.

On the fourth day the carriage reached Bologna. Here the guard handed his letter to the bishop. Wolff, very embarrassed, handed over his letter also. Shamefacedly, he explained that he had read it in order to find out what was going to happen to him. The bishop smiled and told him not to fear, that he would be sent on to Vienna.

While he was in Bologna, Wolff received a letter from Cardinal Litta. The bishop of Bologna had written to this man about Wolff. The cardinal gently rebuked him for his suspicions.

"Don't you know that I have been your friend from the day you arrived in Rome?" he asked. "I tried to protect you in every way I could, but you refused to heed my warnings."

After a time Joseph was sent with another guard to Venice, and finally over the Alps to Vienna. When they arrived there, the guard turned to Wolff, handed him some money, and told him he was free to go wherever he liked. Wolff was overjoyed. Losing no time, he searched out some of the friends he had made in Vienna two years before. They were equally happy to see him.

Then followed another series of adventures. Wolff journeyed from one monastery to another. A rough abbot named Passerat was in charge of one of these establishments. He treated the monks cruelly, and he attempted to treat Wolff the same way.

One day in a fit of anger the big man told Wolff to bow down and kiss his big toe. Wolff bowed all right, only instead of kissing the toe, he bit it so hard that the abbot danced out of the room screaming. Wolff was commanded to get out and never return. With only fifty cents in his pocket, he took to the road with no destination in mind.

As he walked down the street of Lausanne he met a woman. Intuition told him that she was not Swiss. Walking up to her, he asked, "Are you an Englishwoman?"

"Yes, why do you ask?"

"Do you know of a man by the name of Henry Drummond?" She gazed intently at the young man.

"Yes, I do," she answered. Suddenly she held out her hand.

"You must be Joseph Wolff!"

"That's right," he replied.

"For months I have been searching for you. I have a letter for you from Mr. Drummond. You must go to England, where he is waiting for you. Your expenses of traveling to London will be paid for you."

At the hotel where the woman was staying, they found Mr. Thomas Jones. This man accompanied Wolff as far as Paris. From there, Wolff went on with Robert Haldane, another friend of Drummond.

In London he was met by Mr. Drummond, who was overjoyed to see him again.

"Wolff, you *will* become a Protestant now, won't you?" he asked.

"Yes," Wolf replied, "I am not satisfied with the Roman Catholic religion."

"Well, Wolff, you will have to decide for yourself which Protestant church you wish to join."

So Wolff began to *visit* the London churches, a different one every Sunday. After the quietness and reverence of the Catholic cathedrals, he was shocked by the irreverence of Londoners during their church services. One day he visited an Anglican church (called Episcopalian *in* America. All was quiet. He returned many times, enjoyed the sermons, made friends with the minister, and found himself in agreement with the church doctrines. So he joined the Church of England and remained a member for the rest of his life.

All this time he still harbored his dream of becoming a missionary.

"You must become thoroughly grounded in our faith before you can go and preach it to others," said his friend Drummond. He therefore arranged for Wolff to study at Cambridge University for two years. While there, Wolff taught some foreign languages to help earn his board and tuition. But most of the time he read and studied. Often he would get up at two in the morning and read for fourteen hours, with hardly a break for rest or food.

At this time he lived with a man named Simon. One morning when Wolff came to breakfast Simon said to him, "Wolff, go shave off those whiskers. You look like a barbarian!"

The embarrassed Wolff muttered, "I don't know how to shave. I tried, but I could never learn to shave myself."

Simon threw up his hands in amazement.

"Twenty-five years old and never shaved yourself! Come with me to the bathroom. I will teach you."

First he demonstrated how to sharpen the straight-edged razor. Wolff then grasped the strap, but when he began honing his razor, he succeeded only in cutting the strap in two. Simon gave up!

Wolff was very forgetful. One rainy day he needed to attend a lecture, but possessed no umbrella.

"Borrow mine," said Simon. "Just be sure to return it."

Wolff took it, but of course he mislaid it during the day. The next morning Simon had found another one. *This* time he put his name on it.

The next rainy day Wolff again borrowed Simon's umbrella. Again he lost it. Joseph hoped that it might be returned, but he hoped in vain. In despair he asked the housekeeper how he could break the sad news to Simon.

"Write an interesting essay," she said, "and take it to him. Write something you think will please him."

Wolff did so. After Simon had praised the essay, Wolff announced, "Simon, I have some bad news for you."

"Very well, out with it."

"I have lost your second umbrella."

"I am not at all surprised," Simon replied, and with that the matter was closed.

At Cambridge University, Wolff did well in his studies. After two years he was eager to start on his missionary journeys. He asked the Church Missionary Society to send him, but for one reason or another his request was not granted.

Finally Drummond said to him, "Wolff, go anyway. I will pay your expenses."

But Simon spoke up. "I don't think Wolff should leave here until he is able to shave himself."

Drummond laughed and said that he would leave that particular problem up to Wolff.

When the missionary society learned that Drummond planned to send Wolff without their aid, they decided that he should go as their representative. Finally the great day came, the day for which Joseph Wolff had prepared and studied for years, the day that was to mark the beginning of his missionary career.

Armed with letters of introduction, he boarded ship and sailed to Gibraltar, where he had heard there was a large colony of Jews. His great burden was to visit his own people. They must learn of the Saviour, Jesus Christ. They must accept Him as the true Messiah, the one for whom they had been waiting and longing through many centuries.

In what way was Wolff equipped for mission work? He possessed a strong body, one that could resist great variations of cold and heat. As you shall see, this was to prove of immense value to him. He was blessed with a quick and agile mind. He was already acquainted with several foreign languages, including some of the Moslem tongues. He had only two fears. He was afraid to travel by sea, and he was afraid to ride on a horse. Every time he had attempted to mount, he had landed on the ground! In time, however, he was to overcome both of these handicaps.

So Wolff sailed away from England. He was starting on the most adventurous years of his life.

5
Among His
Own People

IT TOOK twenty-two days for the little ship carrying Joseph Wolff to reach Gibraltar. Some days,
of course, were pleasant. On others, fierce gales
sent poor Wolff shuddering to his cabin. The first
of these storms arose very suddenly.

Wolff was sitting on deck reading a book written
by a Jew denouncing Christianity. Almost without
warning a large wave crashed over the side of the
ship, drenching Wolff and nearly washing the book
out of his hands. Seeing black clouds ahead, he
disappeared, not to emerge for two days. When the
sun finally shone again, he made his way to the
captain's cabin and knocked on the door.

"Come in," shouted the captain, with whom
Wolff had made friends on the first day of the voyage. "Glad to see you, Wolff. Feeling better?"

"Much better," Wolff replied. "Now, captain, the
storm is past. Let us kneel down and thank God
for taking it away and for saving us from death."

So there in the cabin they knelt, and Wolff offered up a simple prayer of thanksgiving.

The knelt there in the cabin, and Wolff offered up a simple
prayer of thanksgiving.

A week later, off the coast of Spain, when Wolff was relaxing on deck and reading from that same book, a huge wave came over the side and drenched him again! When Wolff told the captain about it, the officer was surprised.

"Wolff," he said, trying to look stem, "stop reading that book. We don't want any more storms!"

Finally arriving at Gibraltar, Wolff went to see the bishop of the colony. "How many Jews are there in this place?" he asked

"About sixteen hundred, I think," the bishop replied.

These were the people Wolff was most eager to work for. He was positive that he could persuade them to acknowledge Jesus as the Messiah. But the Jews, though quite willing to argue with Wolff, were not interested in becoming Christians.

Said Rabbi Nahimar, "I hear that your intention is to convert the Jews at Jerusalem. You must know that we Jews are attached to our religion. You will find it impossible to convert a Jew."

Wolff replied, "It is true I cannot convert; God only can convert. But I shall tell everyone that I, who was once a Jew, am now a Christian and believe that Jesus is the Messiah."

They had many debates. The Jews on Gibraltar did not believe that Wolff was sincere.

"You speak very well, Wolff," they said, "but deep down inside you are still a Jew."

Wolff left some copies of the Hebrew New Testament with these people, and some of them promised to read it.

From Gibraltar he went to the island of Malta. The bishop there had never heard of a Jew becoming a Christian minister, and he wondered whether Wolff could preach. To prove that he could, Wolff and the bishop entered the empty church, and Wolff preached to the bishop alone. He did so well that the bishop gave him the use of the largest church on the island.

Wolff's next objective was Egypt. He wanted to visit the great city of Cairo. At Alexandria in Egypt he found a sailing ship that would take him up the river. On this boat he met an American by the name of English who had actually become a Mohammedan. Early one morning the two men began talking, and for fourteen hours they continued. During this time Mr. English smoked and ate a few sandwiches but Wolff was so interested in the conversation that he did not stop even for food. That evening when Wolff finished his final appeal, Mr. English burst into tears.

"You have spoken to my heart," he said. "I shall cease to be a Moslem."

Another of Wolff's great desires was to visit Mount Sinai. The British consul in Cairo suggested that he take gifts for the Bedouin chief he would meet in the desert. Wolff managed to find two Englishmen eager to make the journey with him, and on October 29 their camel caravan set out.

Down the Sinai Peninsula they traveled. As the desert heat increased, Wolff thought with pity of the Israelites who long ago had made that same journey.

"Remember, Wolff," said one of his companions, "the children of Israel always had a nice cloud over them to keep off the hot sun."

Finally they were forced by the heat to journey at night, when it was really cool and the stars shone in the clear, black desert sky. Early one morning they saw in the distance the dim outline of a jagged mountain. Their Arab guides told them it was Sinai.

Just as the sun was making further travel uncomfortable, the party arrived at the foot of the mountain. They saw the monastery of St. Catherine perched on one of the high slopes, where monks had been living for hundreds of years.

Wolff looked at the monastery and wondered how they would ever get into it. He could see no door. The guides led them directly beneath a window high up on the wall. When the men shouted, ropes were let down. One by one the visitors were hoisted up into the building. Wolff couldn't help expressing his surprise.

"We must protect ourselves," the monks explained. "You see, the Arabs of this region are not friendly to us." They later explained that in the monastery was an ancient copy of the Bible. The Arabs believed that if in time of drought the monks would open that Bible to the books of Moses and pray for rain, their prayers would be immediately answered. They were constantly ordering the monks to pray for rain, and when it failed to come, they angrily declared that the monks were too lazy to help them.

Wolff always carried a supply of Bibles and Testaments along with him. Some of these he left at the monastery. Fifteen years later, when he visited the place again, he was told that among the visitors who had come during his absence was a Jew from Bulgaria. This man had read one of the Testaments and as a result had be come a Christian. The news made Wolff very happy indeed.

His next ambition was to reach the summit of Sinai. He wanted to follow in the footsteps of Moses. But the monks refused to accompany him up the almost 7,000-foot peak.

"The Arabs will kill us if they find us," they explained. So Wolff himself spoke to the Arabs and found some who would guide him and his two companions up the mountain. When they reached the top, Wolff made them all sit down; then in his loudest voice he stood and proclaimed the Ten Commandments! By night fall they had completed their descent. The three friends wanted to return to the monastery.

"No," said the Arab guides, "you will stay with us until those Christian dogs up there in the monastery pray for rain." So the three were forced to follow the Arabs.

With wild shouts these desert dwellers rushed up under the monastery windows calling, "Dogs, will you pray for rain, or will you not?"

"Children," replied one of the monks, "we pray, but it is in God's hands whether He sends rain or not."

"You dogs, you dogs!" responded the Arabs, shaking their fists at the monks.

Wolff and the other white men were then marched to the Arab camp and thrust into a very old, very black, and very dirty tent, where they remained for several days.

When poor Wolff discovered that his beard was crawling with lice he asked an Arab to shave him, since he had never yet learned to shave himself. The Arab did the job very neatly with a piece of glass. Wolff paid him with a piece of bread and some cheese, and the man seemed quite disappointed. Many years later he found this same Arab and was reminded of that shave. Wolff then gave him a dollar, which satisfied the man at last.

One day the Arab leader spoke to Wolff.

"Sir," he said, "we want you to write to the pasha of Egypt and tell him how bad and lazy these monks are who will not pray for rain." Instead Wolff sent a letter addressed to the British consul telling him how he and his two companions were being kept prisoners by the Arabs. Immediately the consul sent messengers, who ordered the wild desert dwellers to let their captives go. The Arabs obeyed.

Wolff and his companions were a strange sight when they reached Cairo. Down the streets of the city they rode on their camels, wearing a mixture of European and :Arab dress. Many by standers ridiculed and jeered at them as they passed along on their way to the British consulate.

But Mr. Salt, the consul, was very happy to see them. Wolff had a wonderful time at dinner with him that night, relating his experiences on the journey to Sinai. He had always loved to talk, and this time he had more than ever to discuss. In fact, he became so absorbed in his story that when the dish of plum pudding was handed to Wolff, the honored guest, he promptly put the whole thing on his plate and went right on talking.

The other diners were highly amused, particularly Mr. Salt. Not until he had devoured the whole pudding, talking between bites, and gesturing, did Wolff realize what he had done. He was greatly embarrassed.

The next night Mr. Salt invited him again. Once more he got Wolff started talking at a great rate about his adventures among the Arabs. Then just for a joke he handed Wolff a plate containing a whole roast goose. But Wolff had not forgotten. Smiling, he helped himself to one slice, then passed the plate back to his host, remarking, "I have not yet digested the plum pudding!"

Before they parted, Mr. Salt asked, "Where are you going from here?"

Replied Wolff, "I must see Jerusalem, the city of my ancestors."

6

Beaten With
Many Stripes

THE LONG camel caravan passed in single file
through the gates of Cairo, bound for the Holy
Land. Joseph Wolff and his friends were mounted
on camels toward the rear of the procession. Besides
his personal belongings, Wolff as usual was taking
many boxes of Scriptures in various languages.
These he would give to anyone willing to read them.

That night around the campfire Wolff talked to
the Arab servants. They were pleased that he could
talk to them in their own language, and astonished that he knew so much about their prophet,
Mohammed.

In about a fortnight they came to Joppa, and
Wolff stayed with the British consul. In a nearby
community dwelt an ancient Samaritan. This man
did not share the hatred that his ancestors had felt
toward the Jews when Jesus was on earth. Great
was Joseph's happiness when this old man, after
long discussions, decided to be come a Christian.

Twenty-five years later, when Wolff was a minister in a small English town, the nephew of this

old Samaritan came to visit him. While Wolff was walking with him along the road, they met a herd of pigs, animals abhorred by the Samaritans.

"Curse them! Curse them!" the visitor shouted. The men who were driving the pigs were astonished. The next day one of the pigs died, and the men angrily blamed the Samaritan for the loss. When Wolff took up a collection to help the visitor, the congregation demonstrated their feelings by giving only one dollar and forty cents!

Wolff stayed in Joppa until he knew the Syrian language. It took him about three months to learn it! Then he visited Acre and Sidon, ancient cities to the north. He stayed for another three months at a Catholic monastery on Mount Lebanon, where he became proficient in the Syriac dialect. Then as he was returning, a band of robbers attacked him, took his clothes, and left him with only a blanket to wear. The British consul in the next town had to give him another outfit of clothing.

Now Wolff felt prepared to enter Jerusalem. Great was his emotion as he came over the brow of a hill and beheld the city of his fathers spread out before him.

Inside the city he entered an Armenian convent and was given a room. Many visitors flocked to him—Jews, Turks, Armenians, Roman Catholics, Protestants, and heathen. He had great influence over them because he could speak their language. Among them he distributed copies of the New Testament.

He visited all the holy places. He spent a night in Gethsemane, climbed the Mount of Olives, visited Bethlehem, went into the tomb where Jesus is supposed to have lain, and tried to visualize the glory of the morning when He came forth.

He then traveled along the coast past Mount Carmel where Elijah had defied Baal, past Tyre and Sidon, and on toward the great city of Aleppo with its 235,000 people. There he was pleasantly surprised to see many people of different races and beliefs living together in peace and harmony.

The people of Juseea, a little town ten miles from Aleppo, invited Wolff to stay with them. But he knew their way of life, and he feared that the bugs and vermin from their houses would transfer themselves to him, so he decided to stay in the open fields and sleep on the ground.

In the evening the men of Juseea came out to visit with him around his little campfire. Wolff pointed to the stars and spoke to them of the One who made all. They asked him many questions. Suddenly, an earthquake struck. The ground shook. Looking toward the town, by the light of the full moon the visitors from Juseea saw their houses collapsing.

"O our houses, our children, our wives!" they cried in terror. Every few moments another shock filled them with new fear. They started running toward the town to rescue their families. Alas! Most were found dead, buried beneath the ruins of their own homes.

At Aleppo, Wolff found that 60,000 people had been killed by the earthquakes. He attempted to comfort the living, who were wandering about trying to find their loved ones.

"Come," Wolff said to a group huddled together in the market place. "Let us pray."

The poor bewildered people gladly knelt, Mohammedan fashion, with their foreheads touching the ground. Even while Wolff was praying, another violent shock shook the city.

"Merciful Allah, the day of judgment has come!" the inhabitants cried, falling to the ground. Many of them said the earthquake was a punishment for their sins.

Wolff next decided to go to the island of Cyprus.

"You will find no Jews there," he was told.

"I know," Wolff replied."The Jews were driven from the island in the days of the Roman Empire and have not returned."

Still, he went there, and was glad that he did. He found that the fanatical Turkish governor was exterminating the Greek Christians. More than a hundred had already been put to death. Even the archbishop had been dragged to the market place and surrounded by soldiers with long swords.

"You must say, 'Allah is great, and Mohammed is his prophet,' " the soldiers had told him.

"That I cannot and will not say," bravely replied the good bishop.

"Kneel down then," they commanded, drawing their swords. "We shall kill you."

Bravely he knelt and began to pray. While he was interceding with God for himself and for the Turks, the soldiers killed him.

One of the Christians told Wolff about their troubles. He went and talked to the governor in the

Turkish language. This greatly pleased the man, and because Wolff pleaded so hard, he agreed to spare the lives of all the remaining Christians on the island. Wolff sent the children of the brave archbishop to England. There they were educated and grew up to be workers for God.

Wolff wandered on. He came again to Sidon, where there lived an Englishwoman named Lady Hester Stanhope. He sent her his card, indicating that he would accept an invitation to visit with her. She replied with an insulting letter, accusing him of changing his religion from Judaism to Christianity just to win the favor of people who could give him money. Wolff sent a polite, dignified reply.

Lady Stanhope read the letter, brought to her by Wolff's messenger.

"Wait here," she said to the messenger. "I have something to give you." She went into the house, and then came out with a long whip in her hand. With this she proceeded to give the poor servant a terrible beating. Wolff was horrified that a Christian should act in such a manner, more so because Lady Hester was a famous woman, and niece of the prime minister of England.

He came to Damascus, and bought a donkey and hired a man to guide him to a monastery nearby. But the man jumped on the donkey and galloped off. Poor Wolff had to run to keep up, otherwise he would have lost both donkey and guide!

Once more he visited Aleppo, hoping to find it rebuilt. To his surprise, it still lay in ruins. The Arabs living there had not cut their beards or changed their clothing for months, to show their horror and shock over the earthquake.

Now Wolff felt that it was time for him to push on into the East. So he joined himself to a large caravan going to Baghdad. The leader of this caravan was Digeon, an unscrupulous Frenchman. On the way they passed through Haran, and Wolff visited the grave of Terah, Abraham's father, who died there long ago.

Passing through that country, they lost their way. While wandering about, they met a Kurd, one of the fierce Mohammedans of that region. Wolff asked the man if he would guide them on their way. The man agreed to do so for a Spanish *real*. Wolff gave him the coin, and the man started going away. Wolff went running after him.

"Aren't you going to guide us?" he asked.

"No," the man replied grinning. "I don't want to go in the direction you wish to travel."

"Then give me back my money," Wolff demanded.

"If you live until you get your money back, you will never die," taunted the Kurd as he trotted off on his horse.

Suddenly the travelers were surrounded by a whole gang of Kurds. They took the entire party to Guzelli. Wolff tried to talk to them of his mission. But he observed the treacherous Digeon whisper something to the chief. Digeon did not know Wolff understood both Turkish and Arabic.

"This man is a Christian and wants all Moslems to leave their religion," said the wicked Digeon in an undertone.

53

The chief turned to Wolff angrily. "Do you wish to upset our religion?"

"I came here to show you the truth," the missionary replied.

Furiously the chief gave an order. His men seized Wolff and carried him to a nearby log. They lifted his feet high in the air, and with bamboo canes gave Wolff two hundred strokes on the soles of his feet. The pain was excruciating. Then they seized all his possessions. Finally he was tied onto the back of a mule and turned out of the camp, to be carried about all night long, in terrible pain and in the freezing cold.

Next morning when the gate of the town was opened, kind villagers found Wolff. They loosed him and tenderly carried him into town. They took him to a Christian monastery, and he was carefully nursed back to health. But it was three weeks before he could stand on his feet again.

When he was better he decided it was time for him to go on his way.

"But Wolff," protested the astonished monks, "aren't you afraid the Kurds will catch you again?"

"I must go on," Wolff replied. "Paul was beaten five times and I but once so far. I still must have many more troubles before I can equal his record."

"How far will you travel?" they asked.

"Clear to India!"

The monks threw up their hands in horror.

"Impossible! You can never get there. You will die on the way."

"Nevertheless, I shall go on," firmly declared the restless, courageous missionary.

Finally he was tied onto the back of a mule and turned out of camp, in terrible pain and in the freezing cold.

7
Back to England

AS SOON as his feet felt somewhat better, Wolff was eager to be traveling again. He joined a large caravan going down the valley toward Baghdad.

As he went with them he thought many times of his ancestor, Abraham, who passed up this same valley on his way to the land of Canaan nearly four thousand years before.

Because his feet were still tender from the terrible beating the Kurds had given him, he purchased a mule on which to ride. Since there were many soldiers in the caravan, the travelers felt safe from robbers.

The country was very dry, the sun extremely hot, and many of the mules died of thirst. On some days the caravan traveled for fifteen hours. Finally they came to the beautiful oasis of Jalakha. Wolff preached to five thousand people, first in Hebrew, then in Arabic. After resting for two days, the travelers moved on to the city of Mosul, where Wolff stayed with a kind bishop.

One evening this man took Wolff for a walk to see some great mounds.

"These mounds," he told him, "are the ruins of old Nineveh, where Jonah preached. Once one of the greatest cities of the world, it is now nothing but these few big piles." Wolff could not know that within twenty years a Frenchman would begin to dig into these same ruins, and that under all that rubble he would find the beautiful palace of the kings of Assyria.

A few more days' travel brought the caravan to the city of Baghdad on the Euphrates, near the site of ancient Babylon. Wolff was kindly received by a wealthy Arab named Agha Sarkees, who acted as agent for the British Government. He provided Wolff with decent clothing and called in an army surgeon to treat his lacerated feet. But Wolff could not stop preaching. He hobbled to the market place, and for a month preached there to the Jews, at the same time giving away hundreds of Bibles. Next, he sailed down the Euphrates to Basra in a small, round boat of woven reeds.

He then entered Persia. At Bushire he helped the people establish a school. His next stop was Shiraz. This place he never forgot.

One night a wealthy Persian nobleman invited him to meet some friends. They were talking in an upstairs room when a great storm blew up. Clouds of dust flew down the street, followed by pelting rain. Suddenly the house began to rock from side to side, and Wolff knew that it was an earthquake. Remembering what had happened to Aleppo, he ran downstairs and out into the street without taking time to put on his shoes or coat. It turned out to be only a light quake, and his friends urged him to return to the house. But remembering Aleppo, he refused, and slept outside on the wet street! He feared that another shock would demolish the house.

On and on he journeyed, across the bare plain of Persia. At Persepolis he preached to thousands of people among the ruins of the palace where the kings of Persia had dwelt long before.

Many more miles of traveling by muleback brought him to the capital city, Teheran. Here he decided not to go farther east just then, but to turn northward and visit southern Russia. So, joining another caravan, he passed through Tabriz and finally reached Tillis, in the far south of the Russian Empire. This journey took him past a high mountain, the top covered with clouds. His companions told him it was Mount Ararat, where the ark had rested after the Flood.

At Tillis, Wolff became very ill. A kindhearted man took him to a monastery and asked the monks to care for him until he was fully recovered. They agreed, but one priest was so eager to get Wolff to join their company that he argued with the sick man for hours. Finally Joseph, weak as he was, left the house and sat down in the street to get some peace. A British officer took pity on him and led him to his own lodging, and Wolff stayed there until he was well.

At another town he was handed an important-looking letter adorned with heavy seals. Inside he found a message that thrilled him. It was from

the ruler of Russia, Czar Alexander I. It requested Wolff to visit the emperor the next week in a
nearby town. But the meeting never took place, for
within a week the Czar was dead. Wolff went on
into the Crimea, then to Odessa, preaching to the
Jews everywhere, telling them more about Jesus
than they had ever heard before.

From Odessa, Wolff decided to go by ship across
the Black Sea to Constantinople. At the water front
he found a ship called the *Little*. He went on board
to speak to the captain.

"I want to go with you to Constantinople when
you sail next week."

"Who are you?" the captain asked.

"Joseph Wolff, a missionary."

The captain looked him up and down.

"My answer is No! I have always found it brings
bad luck to carry preachers. Besides, my boat is
too *Little!*" he laughed, making a joke out of the
name of his ship.

So Wolff toured the docks until he found another ship, the *Thetis*, whose captain gladly carried
him to Constantinople. Much to his surprise, he
learned a few weeks later that the *Little* had gone
down in a terrible storm on the Black Sea. Not one
person on board had been saved!

At Constantinople he was welcomed by Sir
Stratford Canning, the British consul. Canning
warned him not to leave the house, for it was not
safe for a Christian to be seen on the streets. For
several years Turks and Greeks had been fighting,
and the Turks hated all Christians.

But danger never worried Wolff. One day he slipped out of Constantinople and went to a nearby city where he boldly preached Christ in the market place. Enraged Moslems gathered to kill him, but he escaped half an hour ahead of the soldiers sent to rescue him, and got safely back to Constantinople. Finding he could do nothing further there, Wolff decided he should return to England. He had traveled so widely that little of his mail caught up with him.

So he took ship for Ireland, that being the first port of call. Unfortunately, the winds were unfavorable, and the journey took two long months.

In Dublin, Ireland, Wolff stayed with the archbishop. One of the first things he had to do was tell the archbishop that he could not shave himself, but really would feel more civilized without his whiskers. The archbishop laughed and called in an old woman, who cut off Wolff 's beard with a piece of broken glass. As soon as he looked presentable, Wolff began preaching, and many people came to hear him.

Soon a letter arrived from his friend Henry Drummond. "My dear Wolff," it said, "you have returned from your travels but have not come to London. I am most anxious to see and talk with you again."

So Wolff sailed across the Irish Sea, and by stagecoach went to London. He was first taken to the home of Edward Irving, England's greatest preacher at that time. Irving received him joyfully. "Get ready quickly, Wolff," he said. "We are going out to dinner tonight."

Wolff had no fashionable clothing such as was worn to dinner parties, so Irving lent him an outfit. Looking very fine, the two left by coach for the party. They were speedily driven to the home of Lady Olive Sparrow, where Wolff met a group of famous people.

As they surrounded the banquet table the attention of all the guests was focused on the man who had traveled through such far away lands. All were eager to hear of his adventures. But for once Wolff found it hard to talk. Directly across the table from him sat a lovely young woman, Georgiana Walpole, the daughter of the earl of Oxford, a wealthy and powerful man. Poor Wolff thought he had never seen anyone so beautiful, and immediately fell in love with her. He found it difficult to see or talk with anyone else at the table. Late that night, on the way home, he kept asking Irving all about the Lady Georgiana.

Before retiring, Wolff was obliged to confess to Irving the same thing he had told the archbishop in Dublin.

"Irving," he began, "do you think you could send a servant tomorrow morning to shave me?"

Irving looked astonished.

"Do you mean to say," he began, "that you have never——"

"That's right," Wolff interrupted hastily. "I have never learned how to shave myself. I have tried to learn several times but never have succeeded."

"Very well," replied Irving, "someone will come."

True to his word, someone did come. Next morning there was a rap on the bedroom door.

When Wolff opened it, he beheld Edward Irving, England's greatest preacher, wearing an apron and carrying shaving brush, mug, and razor. In a few minutes the task was completed.

Irving continued to come every morning as long as Wolff remained in his house. The servants knew about it, and soon all London had heard and was laughing at what they thought was a wonderful joke. But Wolff said he knew how Peter felt when Jesus washed his feet.

One day Wolff and Irving were walking together up Oxford Street. A crowd of people stood outside a shop window greatly amused by something. The two men elbowed their way into the crowd, and beheld a painting hanging in the window. It showed Edward Irving sitting down holding a huge, fierce wolf between his knees, and he was busy shaving off the beast's whiskers! When the crowd recognized the two men looking at the picture, they laughed harder than ever.

"Never mind, Wolff," Irving said, taking his arm. "I will shave you again." And he did, several times.

A few days later Wolff went with Irving to an important conference of preachers from all over England. As they studied the prophecies, especially those of Daniel, they all became convinced that Jesus was coming back to the earth soon. Now Joseph Wolff was possessed of a new desire-to carry that wonderful news to the great countries of Asia.

All during these weeks he was becoming better acquainted with Miss Walpole. Alone one day he asked her to be his wife. Great was his joy when she consented. Her father, the old earl, was not so happy.

"What kind of home can a wandering Jew like you provide for my lovely daughter?" he asked. "She is very rich, as you know, and what do *you* have?"

But Wolff did not covet Lady Walpole's money. He therefore wrote out a statement declaring that he never wanted a penny be longing to her. Reluctantly, after a very long time, the old earl consented to the wedding, and they were married in a fashionable London church.

A few months after the wedding Wolff began to be restless again. He announced to his bride that he was planning another trip to Asia.

"Very well, Joseph," she said, "but you must understand that I shall go with you."

Overwhelmed with surprise, Wolff could only stare at her. He thought of some of the dreadful places he had been, and of some of the even more dreadful places he still planned to visit. But he knew it was useless to argue with his Lady Georgiana.

"All right," he replied, "you may come with me until you decide in your own mind that it would be better for you to stay in England"

"Wherever you go, Joseph, I will go."

"That remains to be seen."

And the matter was closed.

So in the year 1827 Joseph Wolff and his young bride sailed from England to Amsterdam. He was setting out on his longest and most dangerous journey, one that would keep him from England for more than five years.

8

In Perils by Sea

SOON after he began this journey, Wolff reached the town where he had been born, and he wondered whether he would find any of his relatives still living. To his great joy, he found both his mother and his sister. He had not seen them for eighteen years.

"Today I have been born again," sobbed the mother, her tears flowing freely down her weathered cheeks as she embraced her son.

Many of the Jews in this town had known him and his father, and Wolff announced that he would preach to them. Filled with curiosity to hear this world-famous Christian missionary, they flocked to his meetings. Of course, his mother and sister came also.

How intensely Wolff prayed and struggled to convert his dear ones! To his great joy, he won his sister; but the old mother refused to believe that her husband, good Rabbi David, had been wrong in any of his beliefs. She clung to the old Jewish ways.

For some months Wolff and his wife traveled around Europe, after which they sailed for the island of Malta. Wolff could not get Asia out of his mind. There were still so many wild, desolate, dangerous areas to visit in those lands ruled by the Moslems. He knew he would find many Jews in those regions.

At Malta they stopped for a time, and a little son was born. Leaving his new family in the care of kind friends, Wolff started out alone on a visit to Greece and Asia Minor. At Smyrna he distributed hundreds of Bibles, even to the Turks. At Corfu, one of the islands in the Aegean Sea, the crowds were so dense that he had to preach in the streets.

As he traveled across the Greek mainland he beheld the terrible desolation left by the Turks. At Navarino Bay he saw wrecked Egyptian warships sunk in a naval battle and met a famous British soldier, Sir Charles Napier.

"So you are the man who thinks the end of the world is coming in 1845," remarked Sir Charles.

"No, sir," Wolff replied, "not in 1845, but in 1847." (As you know, in America the return of Jesus was expected in 1844.)

Returning to Malta, Wolff joined his wife and son. Together they sailed to Alexandria in Egypt, where many of Wolff's old friends lived. They sailed by way of Cyprus, where a wonderful welcome awaited them. Those Christians had never forgotten how Wolff had saved them from the swords of the Turks, or how he had comforted the orphaned children of their archbishop, who had been killed in the market place. Thousands flocked to hear him.

But sorrow and trouble also awaited them on Cyprus. First, Wolff's wife became very ill, then their baby boy died and had to be buried there. Georgiana began to wonder whether it would be best for her to follow Joseph on all of his wanderings. Together the two returned to Cairo. There Joseph purchased camels, loaded them with Bibles, joined a caravan, and went up to Jerusalem.

On his first visit to that place he had found the Jews very friendly. But this time they were hostile, looking the other way when he came along, and refusing to greet him on the street. He wondered what had changed them, until he learned that the Jews in Europe had written to their friends in Jerusalem, instructing them to have nothing to do with Wolff.

While in Jerusalem, Wolff and his wife stayed with a Dr. Stomont. Wolff warned this man to be careful how he pushed his way into the holy places of the Jews. But Dr. Stomont thought he knew better. One day while he was inspecting the stones from the ruins of the old Temple of Solomon, the Jews seized him, stripped him of nearly all his clothing, and locked him in a cow shed.

Hour after hour Dr. Stomont cried, "Wolff! Wolff! Wolff!" People who heard his cries reported the matter to Wolff, who went to the Jewish court and bribed some of the clerks with money. Reluctantly the magistrate ordered Stomont to be released. Perhaps Dr. Stomont was glad to be set free, but he never gave Wolff anything for all the money Wolff had spent obtaining his freedom. In fact, he refused to repay him.

Since the people of Jerusalem would not listen to his message, the Wolffs sailed back to Alexandria.

Here Joseph did a very bold but a very unwise thing. He wrote a message to the Mohammedan governor of the city. Among other things, he told the man, "Mohammedan power in Egypt is going to fall. You have only one thing to do. Repent and believe on Jesus."

Wolff told a certain Arab to carry this message to the governor. Of course, the governor became furious and gave orders that Wolff's messenger should be flogged. This, in turn, made the poor messenger very angry. After his beating he sought out the missionary and threatened to give him a beating in return. Wolff gave him two dollars to make him feel better. After that, whenever the man saw Wolff walking about the city, he would shout, "Never send me with another message of such rubbish to the governor again!"

"But I gave you two dollars for doing it," responded Wolff. "You should have given me ten dollars," growled the man, still angry.

The governor complained to the British consul about this mistake Wolff had made. The consul ordered Wolff to leave, but allowed his wife to remain. The husband and wife were separated, and Wolff sailed to the island of Rhodes. There were many Turks in this place, and when Wolff's servant foolishly left his master's case open, the Turks saw that it was full of Bibles and became enraged, which troubled Wolff not at all.

One afternoon as he was sailing in a little boat along the shore of Greece, some of the sailors pointed to a strange boat that was rapidly overtaking them. The men were filled with alarm. They knew by the flag at the masthead that this was a pirate ship, an especially dreaded variety, whose crew frequently killed every person they captured.

Some of the terrified sailors threw themselves into the sea. Wolff and his servant followed their example. They managed to reach shore, scrambled out of the water, and fled into a forested mountain area. Since Wolff was without shoes or coat, his feet were soon filled with terrible thorns, and his shirt was torn to shreds. In the intense heat he suffered severely, being without drinking water.

Just when it seemed that Wolff and his servant must die, they came upon some shepherds who took them to a hut, washed their feet, bound up their wounds, and gave them food and drink. Then one of the men guided them over mountain trails to Salonika, the Thessalonica of Bible times, where the apostle Paul had preached. Wolff had been so badly injured by the thorns that he had to remain there for many weeks, until he had removed the last of them from his feet.

Then he sailed for Malta, where he rejoiced to find his wife and a second son, already several weeks old. One day, after he had traced on a map the various cities of Asia he wished to visit, Georgiana sadly agreed that she and their little son could not safely make such a journey. So in a few days she and her baby boarded a ship bound for England. Joseph told her plainly that she might never see him again. Although she was proud of her brave missionary husband, these words made her very sad. It was not easy for Wolff, either. With tear-dimmed eyes he stood on the dock watching until her ship had completely disappeared.

Soon Wolff began his journey. First he went to Constantinople to obtain travel permits. His financial needs had been cared for by the governor of Malta, who had lent him three thousand dollars. The Turks agreed to issue him permits, but pointed out that in many of the countries he planned to visit they had but little authority. In spite of this discouraging information, he bought a horse, hired an Armenian servant, and set out once more. Again he carried with him many boxes full of Bibles and Testaments in various languages.

They passed through Asia Minor and on to the shores of the Black Sea. There Wolff found a beautiful red sedan chair sent by the British consul to carry him to Astara. In that place, as usual, he preached to a large congregation, constantly working his way to Teheran, the capital of Persia. The people tried to persuade him not to continue his journey.

"Where do you want to go, Wolff?" they asked him.

"I am going to Bokhara," he replied, "and I should like to know the safest route."

"You cannot go safely," was the answer.

"Why not?"

"Because they will kill you in Khorasan, for they cannot bear Christians. And if you should slip safely through Khorasan and arrive at Sarakhs, where there are six thousand tents of Turkomans, they will keep you a slave. And if you slip through Sarakhs safely and arrive in Merv, you will still be in the same danger. And if you slip safely through Merv and arrive in Bokhara, you will either be kept there and never be allowed to leave, or you will be killed, as they killed Morcroft and Guthrie and Trebek six years ago, even though the Englishmen gave them many presents. Not only that, but you have physical troubles. You are so shortsighted that you cannot see when robbers are coming."

To this Wolff replied calmly, "God is mighty above all things. He will take care of me."

Walking around the market place looking for a caravan that might be going toward Bokhara, Wolff found an Afghan who was traveling that way. This man agreed to guide him to Bokhara. Then Wolff noticed a white spot just below the man's ear.

"What is that sore on your neck?" he asked.

"Just a little leprosy," the man calmly replied.

Wolff immediately lost all interest in traveling with him!

He soon found a caravan going halfway to Bokhara. Thinking this was better than making the trip alone, Wolff bought four camels, loaded them with his Bibles, hired two Persian servants, and set out. He was soon to realize that both of these Persian servants were rascals.

For the first four days all went well. Then, ahead of them, blocking their path, they beheld nearly a thousand Turkoman warriors. Fearfully the caravan halted, debating what to do. Wolff was told that it was the custom of the Turkomans to

Boldy Wolff advanced to meet them, and thinking
of the plague the Turkoman warriors galloped
back to their company.

attack all caravans, kill some of the travelers, rob all, and make slaves of the living.

The main body of the Turkomans did not advance. A handful of the warriors, however, rode forward, inquiring where the caravan had come from and where it was going.

"We are from Teheran, and we are on our way to Burchund," replied the leader of Wolff's caravan. "Is not the plague raging in Teheran?" asked the leading Turkoman, backing away from people whom he feared might infect him and his men with the plague.

Boldly Wolff advanced alone to meet them. Thinking more of the plague than anything else, the Turkoman warriors wheeled and galloped back to their company. Soon the entire group disappeared in the distance.

9
Face to Face With Mohammedanism

WITH relief the members of the caravan watched the Turkoman warriors ride away toward the mountains. They crowded around Wolff and praised him, for they were positive that by some magic he had frightened the enemies away. Then they went on peacefully to the city of Boostan. In amazement the people of that place came out to meet them.

"How did you get here?" they questioned. "We came along the road."

"Didn't you see any Turkomans on the way? "

"We saw hundreds of them, but they did not molest us."

"You were lucky. They are everywhere these days. If you leave this town they will take you prisoner."

Hearing this, the caravan leader wanted to stay in Boostan, but Wolff wanted to depart. He had only begun his long journey to Bokhara, Afghanistan, and India. He was carrying a letter from the king of Persia, instructing all the king's servants to protect him. Armed with this letter, Joseph went to the governor. When the astonished man saw who had written it, he bowed his head and kissed it.

"What do you want?" he asked Wolff.

"I want to go to Bokhara."

"Very well, I will send you safely. But first you must give me a paper promising that the king of England will give me a pension of $15,000 a year!"

The astonished missionary protested. "I could never do that! And the king of England would never pay you the money even if I did sign such a paper!"

"Very well,"' replied the governor. "Go where you like and when you like, but I shall not protect you." And he sent Wolff out of the palace.

In the market place Wolff found two men who were going to the next town, and they agreed to let him go with them. So the two little companies joined forces and started out. After two days they came to Burchund. The men insisted on stopping. They dared travel no farther, for the country ahead was overrun with robbers. So with his servants and camels Wolff proceeded alone.

Soon he heard the sound of galloping horses behind him. These were not robbers but soldiers sent to bring Wolff back to the ruler of Burchund for questioning. This man feared that Wolff had come to his country as a spy.

"Who are you?" he asked when Wolff stood before him.

"I am a Christian missionary." "Where do you come from?" "England."

"Where are you going?"

"To Bokhara."

"Why do you go around the country like this when you might be at home with your wife and family?"

Wolff replied that he wanted to share with others the wonderful joy that was his in knowing Jesus Christ. He then read a passage from his Bible to the ruler and his counselors.

"A man of God, indeed!" they all cried out. "Drunk with the love of God! Oh, why do we not repent?"

After that they treated him very kindly. He stayed two weeks in the city. Many of the inhabitants accepted his Bibles, and he often saw them being read in the market place.

But Wolff still wanted to reach Bokhara. When he found a small company going on to the next town, he joined them. It was now winter. The ground was covered with snow. Wolff was riding about a quarter of a mile ahead of the group when suddenly he heard shooting, then shouting and screaming.

Quickly he rode back, only to discover that a band of robbers had captured the whole company. Many of the men had already been stripped and tied onto the backs of their own horses. The bandits did the same to Wolff, then drove the whole company off the road and up to a mountain cave that was their headquarters.

One of the bandits asked Wolff who he was.

"I am a follower of Jesus."

Now, the Mohammedans believe that Jesus was a prophet but not the Son of God. So when they heard that name they untied Wolff, after which the whole company, prisoners and robbers, entered the cave together. The robbers broke into Wolff's boxes, seized his food parcels, and began to eat greedily, without offering a bite to Wolff or his servants.

The robbers discussed the amount of money they should receive when they sold their captives into slavery. Pointing to Wolff, one man stated, "I think he is worth about ten dollars." His companion laughed. "Nobody would give more than five for such a man as he!"

They next began investigating Wolff's clothing. They pounced upon his supply of money, and found the letter from the king of Persia. This made them afraid.

"The king will become angry if he hears that we have captured an Englishman."

"Then let us kill him. If anyone asks, we can say that the Turkomans killed him."

"There is no use doing that," Wolff broke in. "Before leaving the last city I sent different messengers to the prince, saying that if I did not reach Bokhara he would know that I had been captured by robbers."

Now the robbers began to tremble.

"You must give us everything you have," they said.

"That is all right. I care nothing for the things of this world. Besides, if you will take me to Torbad

Hydarea, the Jews there will raise even more money as a ransom for me."

To this the robbers agreed. Wolff and his servants were escorted to the town. The Jews looked with pity upon the penniless, poorly clad missionary as he stood shivering in the deep snow, and they implored the robbers to allow him to spend the night with them. With the consent of the thieves, they gave him some clothing. Then they asked him about Jesus, the Son of God. Most of that night Wolff, cold and ragged, spoke to them of the Saviour.

In the morning the robber chief returned, seized Wolff, and threw him into a dungeon with many other captives, shouting as he strode off, "I hope you are comfortable now!" Poor Wolff wondered whether he would ever be able to resume his journey. Perhaps the robbers planned to starve him to death in this dreadful place.

About two hours later he was startled to hear the sound of guns being fired. Soon a fierce-looking soldier unlocked the dungeon. Wolff was told that the governor of the country had returned, and had surprised and overpowered the robbers.

The governor, a large, powerful man, summoned Wolff to his court. On one side huddled Joseph's tormentors, guarded by fierce soldiers.

"I am a man of justice," the governor announced. "Now you will see my justice. Tell me, Wolff, how much money did these robbers steal from you?"

"Eighty tomans." (About two hundred dollars.)

"Eighty tomans?"

"Very well." The guards took from the robbers all the money they had in their possession, including Wolff's eighty romans.

"Now you shall see my justice."

The governor ordered the robbers to be flogged. Then he put the whole sum of money into his own pocket, and Wolff was sent penniless out of the courtroom.

He stayed with the Jews at Torbad Hydarea until he heard of a caravan journeying toward Bokhara. This he gladly joined. The first day out of town the caravan managed to beat off a band of robbers. At Meshed, Wolff preached to the Jews about Jesus. Here he met an English captain who gave him money and clothing. During the two months he spent at Meshed he won the respect of all its people. Then he heard that a large caravan, made up of many horses and camels, was leaving soon for Merv and Bokhara. Eagerly he joined it.

Traveling with him were two boys, captured to be sold at Bokhara into slavery. As they trudged along they sang this sad song:

> The Al Amman have taken us,
> Poor, poor Guzl Boash,
> To carry us and carry us
> In irons and chains, irons and chains
> To Organtsh and Bokhara.

At Merv, Wolff visited the market place and found many slaves being sold at auction. He purchased several and immediately set them free to return to their homes.

One day they came to the Oxus River, which was deep and wide. Only one frail boat was available to carry all the people across. Wolff had endured so many dangers that he was very nervous. When the boat rocked up and down in that swift river, he thought it would surely tip over and throw him into the icy water. He began to scream.

"Don't worry," one of his companions said. "Just sit down and I will help you."

He then blindfolded Wolff. Since he could no longer see the danger, this calmed him, and the whole caravan safely reached the opposite shore.

One beautiful morning the caravan rode into Bokhara, the city toward which Wolff had been traveling for more than a year.

During the following days Wolff preached to both Jews and Mohammedans. But Bokhara was still not the end of his journey. He wanted to travel through Afghanistan and down into India. There he knew he could find a ship to take him back to England.

"Wolff, you are mad," the Jews told him. "No Christian would dare go through Afghanistan. It would mean certain death." But nothing could stop Wolff once his decision was made. So, when he found a caravan of Afghan merchants he asked to join them.

"If you come with us and we meet some Dooabs, you must say you are a Mohammedan," they told him. Of course, Wolff would never agree to this.

When they reached the country called Dooab, they met one of the fiercest of all Mohammedan tribes. On the journey Wolff's companions had called him hadji, or holy man, because he had been to Jerusalem, a holy city to the Moslems. But these fierce Dooabs believed that only if a person had been to Mecca could he be called hadji.

"Why do you allow this company to call you hadji when you are not a Mohammedan?" they asked rudely.

"The Mohammedans of Bokhara call any man hadji who has been to Jerusalem."

"We do not."

"All right," agreed Wolff. "I shall tell my companions not to call me hadji any more."

"It's too late. Unless you are willing to say, 'There is God and none but God, and Mohammed is the prophet of God,' we will sew you up in a dead donkey, burn you alive, then make sausages of you."

Of course, Wolff knew they were asking him to say that he would become a Mohammedan. This he would never do. As those fierce men closed in around him his companions of the caravan fled, certain they would never behold him alive again. Wolff was shoved into a large cave, and in that dark cavern his captors began to argue whether to put him to death, and if they did, by what means.

Wolff himself had often wondered whether he would reach India alive. In case he failed he had given his caravan leader letters to be sent from India to England, telling his wife that he had fallen a victim to the Afghans. There in that gloomy place this possibility became very real to him, and he began to despair of seeing his wife and little boy again.

Suddenly a bold thought came to him. Striding directly into the midst of the council, he announced, "What no is this? You cannot kill me! It would be against your law, which says you must show hospitality to strangers. You must send me to Mohammed Murad Beyk."

"Do you know him?" they asked, trembling to hear the name of this powerful ruler.

"That you must find out for yourselves," Wolff boldly replied.

"If we release you, give us everything you have," they shouted.

"That I will gladly do, for I care nothing for money or clothing or any other possessions."

They stripped him of everything he possessed and turned him loose. Shivering and penniless, he still had six hundred miles to travel through deserts and valleys and over high mountain passes deep with snow.

10
India at Last

SHIVERING, Joseph Wolff walked out of the cave and away from the fierce Dooab people, who had stripped him of everything but life itself.

His caravan companions never expected to see him again, for they knew how the Moslems hated Christianity. As they journeyed along they discussed Wolff, saying what a good man he was, and expressing sorrow that he was not a Mohammedan.

Suddenly they heard shouting. Turning, they saw Wolff running, trying to catch up. Amazed, they halted and waited for him.

How happy they were! To them it was a miracle that he had escaped from the fierce Dooabs. They crowded closely around him. Their leader commanded them all to bow down in Mohammedan fashion, their foreheads touching the ground, while he offered a prayer. This is what that Mohammedan caravan leader prayed:

> O God, O God, thanks be to Thy name
> That Thou hast saved this stranger,
> Out of the lions' den. Thank! Thanks! Thanks!

Thanks
Be to Thy holy name.
Bring him back safely
Unto his country, unto his family.
Amen, amen.

However, although they pitied him, they gave him no clothing. Wolff wondered how he would be able to exist, walking in mid winter for six hundred miles over high mountain passes and across hot deserts. Fortunately, he was blessed with a strong body, otherwise he would surely have died.

When the caravan came to another town, he went to see the governor, and the man kindly agreed to give him a letter to give to the ruler of the next large town. This is what he wrote: "The man who brings you this letter is Joseph Wolff, an ambassador. Please help him on safely to Kabul."

At Ghuzni, Wolff went to the governor's house, even though he felt embarrassed because of his appearance. He handed the letter to the governor. When the man had finished reading it, he stood amazed. With outstretched arm he pointed to Wolff and began shouting.

"What! A ragamuffin like you without decent clothes! Do you expect me to believe that you are an ambassador?"

Although Wolff tried hard to explain what had happened, the governor refused to listen, and ordered him out of town.

On and on the caravan traveled, stopping by night in different Afghan villages, where Wolff would speak kindly to the people, reminding them of Abraham, the father of all the Arabs, and his kindness to strangers. Sometimes they would take him into their houses, allowing him to sleep near the fire. In the cold early dawns they might, out of pity, give him a chunk of black bread and some milk.

As they began to ascend high mountains, the snow became deeper. Poor Wolff had no animal to ride. Many times he sank into snowdrifts up to his neck. His friends then would stop and pull him out. Finally, when they had crossed the highest pass, they made their way down the other side into a land with a milder climate.

At last they reached a village only a few miles from Kabul, the capital of Afghanistan. Wolff knew there might be English officers there, but he did not want to be seen as he was. So he sent a messenger ahead with instructions to tell the governor, and also any Englishmen he might meet, that Wolff would be arriving soon.

In a little while the messenger and an Afghan came riding back, leading a third horse on which Wolff was to ride into the city. There was also a letter for him from an Englishman by the name of Burnes, who had arrived only the night before, en route to Bokhara. Since Wolff had come from that city, the man was eager to learn about the condition of the road.

Wolff also was handed a basket of clothes, a gift from the ruler. A short while later, clad in these Afghan garments, he rode into Kabul.

While there he stayed with the king's brother, who asked him many questions. He also had many visits with the English traveler. "Wolff, are there any Christians in Bokhara?" the man asked.

"There are at least twenty, because I baptized that many Jews while I was there. They fully accepted Jesus Christ as their Messiah."

"Where do you plan to go from here?"

"I am on my way to India, passing down the Khyber Pass to Peshawar."

The Englishman became very excited.

"Listen!" he exclaimed, "if you go through Peshawar, you will probably meet a rascal there, a real scoundrel by the name of Abdul Samut Khan. For my sake, when you meet him, take him by the shoulders and kick him down the stairs."

We may think it strange, but Wolff promised he would do so! After a month in Kabul, Joseph had regained the strength lost during the terrible hardships he had endured. The king summoned him several times for visits at the palace. Then with his faithful servant he resumed his journey to Peshawar. He had not forgotten his promise to the Englishman, and wondered whether he would meet the evil Abdul Samut Khan. He went to the inn at Peshawar and requested a place to stay.

"I am sorry, sir," replied the innkeeper, "but I have only one room fit for an Englishman to use, and it is already occupied."

"Who is in it, and when is he leaving?" Wolff asked.

"It is occupied by Abdul Samut Khan."

"The very man I am looking for!" exclaimed Wolff, bounding past him up the stairs. The owner followed, pointing out the door of the desired room. Wolff's knock at the door was answered by one of the most ferocious-looking villains he had ever seen. This man opened the door a little crack. But the small and muscular Wolff just pushed his way into the room.

"Do you know Sahib Burnes?" Wolff asked.

"Yes, I know him well," the man growled.

Certain that this was the right person, Wolff seized him by the shoulders, marched him to the door, and shoved him down the stairs! He then took possession of the room. Neither man ever forgot this meeting and many years later Wolff was to pay dearly for his hasty and unwise action.

The traveler next crossed another mountain range, journeying on down into India. There his fortunes swiftly changed.

Many English and Indian people went out of their way to show him kindness and respect. He was even given an elephant to ride, though he feared being so high in the air. One day he had to cross a suspension bridge over a deep chasm. He covered his face with his hands, fearful that the swaying bridge would collapse under the heavy weight of his elephant.

On the outskirts of India's largest city near the Afghan border, Wolff was met by an Indian army officer.

"Who are you?"

"I am Joseph Wolff, the missionary."

One day he had to cross a suspension bridge, and he feared the bridge would collapse under the weight of the elephant.

When this news was flashed back to the fort, twenty-one cannons boomed a salute. As they passed through the gate, Wolff was handed a cash gift that amounted to about sixty dollars in American money. He was also presented with twenty pots filled with sweetmeats, and enough cloth to make twenty new shirts. The soldiers saluted him as the great priest from England, and handed him letters from the governor-general of all India. He was also told that several of his wife's relatives living in India were eager to meet him.

All through India, royal honors were showered upon him. But as often as he could, he called the people together and preached, always telling them of the soon coming of Jesus. Even when he reached the strongly Moslem city of Lahore, he was not afraid to try to spread Christianity. In the market place he put up a notice calling on all nations to repent and return to Christ. It made the ruler of the city so angry that he asked Wolff to move on.

At Amritsar the traveler lodged in the governor-general's house. The first night he was there he was handed a letter containing a check equivalent to more than five hundred dollars! Now he would be able to repay the many strangers from whom he had borrowed money while on his long journey.

In another city he was invited to the palace to meet the prince of a large state. Before visiting such a great man, Wolff decided to shave off his beard. The Indians protested, saying that the people had great respect for any man who could grow such a long beard! "But mine is *very* long!" Wolff protested, "and it hasn't been combed for months."

"Never mind, they will like you all the better for wearing it," he was told. So with his foot-long reddish tangled beard, he was taken to see the prince.

After this visit he continued his journey across India. He found and visited his wife's relatives. What a thrill it was for him when they placed in his hands a letter from Georgiana! He had not seen her for more than two years.

He became eager to behold the beautiful Vale of Kashmir, though he realized that white people were not usually permitted there. But because he was so famous, he received a special invitation from the king of Kashmir to visit him. And as a special favor he was allowed to preach to thousands of people who had never heard of Christ before.

Before leaving, Wolff asked one favor of the king. Hundreds of poor Kashmiri shawl weavers desired permission to move to India. Joseph interceded in their behalf, and as a result the king granted them this privilege. News of this spread far and wide.

When Wolff, with hundreds of these poor weavers, reached the frontier of India, he was stopped by the police. Stepping out of his palanquin—an enclosed litter used for riding—Joseph demanded in a haughty tone, "Do you dare disturb the companions of the great Englishman?"

This frightened the police so much that they took to their heels, and the whole party successfully crossed the border.

At Delhi, the missionary was taken to see the Grand Mogul, a fabulously wealthy ruler. This man gave Wolff clothes all embroidered with jewels. He invited Wolff to remain in India, offering to give him a fine house.

Wolff replied, "I shall presently mount my wooden horse [ship] to take me over the sea—What do I see? The ship takes in her anchor. No time is to be lost, for Christ is to be preached everywhere. Farewell."

At another city he was challenged to discuss his religion with some wise Mohammedan mullahs, or priests. The ensuing discussion lasted for two days, and an Englishwoman who was present reported that Wolff won a great victory. Evidently the prince thought so too, for he gave Wolff a present amounting to ten thousand dollars.

At last he reached the great city of Calcutta. There he preached to twelve hundred people in the town hall. But many more wanted to hear him, so he arranged for them to meet in a quiet field nearby, where he preached twelve hours a day for six days! His audience numbered as many as a thousand people at times. Truly Wolff was a strong man, and he must have been a persuasive speaker.

He then began to retrace his steps across India, preaching all the way. Most of the time he traveled by palanquin. One night as he was moving along, a tremendous rainstorm came up. The water in the swamp through which his group was passing became quite deep. Suddenly and without warning, his carriers set the palanquin down and fled into the darkness. Poor Wolff could do nothing but sit there the rest of the night, the water reaching at times up to his chest. Next morning the bearers returned, looking rather ashamed of their cowardice.

At last, the heat, the cold, and all the sufferings Wolff had endured, proved too much for even his strong body. He became very ill. Fortunately, he was near a city where an English doctor was working. This man told Wolff that he had cholera, and could not hope to live more than a day or two. The disease progressed rapidly, and finally the doctor told him frankly that in all probability he would not live through the night.

"Is there nothing more you can do for me, doctor?" poor Wolff begged. "I do so much want to see my family once more."

"There is only one remedy that I know of," replied the doctor, "but it is such a harsh one that I cannot recommend it."

"Tell me what it is," whispered the dying patient.

"It is one used by the Indian doctors. They put hot irons on your stomach and burn you severely."

"Try it, please, doctor, try it," begged Wolff. "I can only die anyway."

So that night he was branded three times. Strange to say, the cholera immediately left him, though it is doubtful that it was as a result of the treatment.

While he was in a stupor he did not even know when the house in which he was lying caught fire, nor when friends came to his rescue and transferred him to another house nearby. Not until twelve years later, in London, did he learn—from this same doctor—about the fire.

When Joseph regained consciousness, he found that his pain had gone (except for the burns) but he was very weak. He determined to board the first ship sailing for England and return once more to his family and friends.

11
Witness to
All the World

THOUGH Wolff was still convalescing, the doctor plainly told him that he should leave India as soon as possible. From Goa he sailed for Alexandria, Egypt. There he found many friends who remembered his previous visits to Egypt.

From India, Wolff had written to his wife, telling her of his plans to return home. When she received that letter, Georgiana decided to surprise him. She succeeded very well, too. When his ship reached the island of Malta, the place made famous by the ship wreck of Paul, who should be waiting on the dock to welcome him but his beloved wife! Together they returned to England on what almost seemed like a second honeymoon. In England they spent many happy months together.

Lady Georgiana began to notice the old restlessness coming over her husband once more. She began to notice maps lying on his desk, especially maps of Africa.

"Joseph," she asked wistfully, "what are your plans now? Are you going to leave me again?"

"I hope to make a visit to Abyssinia," he replied with a smile.

"Surely, Joseph, after all you have endured, your love for adventure should be satisfied. I had so hoped you would now be able to find happiness here in England."

"It isn't the love of adventure, Georgiana," Wolff replied gently, taking her hand. "How can I settle down here in England when there are thousands and millions of people in Asia and Africa who have never heard the name of Jesus?"

She saw that it would be of no use to try to keep him back. So once again the day came when she watched him sail away to Malta. Georgiana must now again depend on Joseph's infrequent letters to comfort her in her loneliness.

From Malta he went to Alexandria, where he found a ship passing down the Red Sea. As Wolff sailed along the Arabian coast his imagination was captured by the two cities of Mecca and Medina, the holy cities of Mohammedanism. No Christian had been allowed to visit either of them all through the centuries.

At a city in southern Arabia, Wolff went ashore and began talking to the people in the market place. As he had done in so many other places, he visited the emir, to tell him of his travels, and then of the wonderful gospel story. The emir liked this white man.

"Wolff, where are you going from here?" he asked.

"I expect to cross the sea and visit Abyssinia."

The emir raised both hands.

94

"Oh, that you must not do! It would be very dangerous. There are many robbers, and you would surely be killed!"

"Do you not understand that I shall have the help of God? You know that you yourself go around among wild Arabs, and they obey you."

"Ah, yes, but then, you see, I am protected and provided with arms."

"So am I."

"What sort of arms do you carry?"

"Prayer and zeal for Christ are my arms, and also the love of Christ in my heart. It helps me to make friends with other people."

"I have nothing to say to that," replied the emir, who admired Wolff all the more, after that.

Wolff soon found a ship sailing across the Red Sea to a town on the African coast. From there he followed the caravan trail into Abyssinia. But at Adowa he found a missionary whose wife and child were very ill. Though he wanted to go on, he laid aside his plans and stayed and nursed the sick ones for three months. Then he took them down to the nearest seaport, bought tickets with his own money, and sent them off on a sea voyage to help them recuperate. Although a singular man in many ways, Wolff always endeavored to practice the golden rule.

Again he turned his steps toward Abyssinia. As he traveled along he had a strange experience. In one of the towns a man suddenly began to shout. People came running from all directions.

"It is our Aboona! It is our Aboona!" they cried, pointing to Wolff's long beard.

The Aboona is the patriarch of the Abyssinian Church, the spiritual father of millions of Christians living in that land. When traveling around the country, he frequently goes in secret so the people won't bother him with their troubles.

"I am not your Aboona," Wolff declared. They only shouted the more. In a desperate effort to convince them, he somehow got hold of a pipe and took a few puffs, a thing no patriarch would ever do.

"You are only doing that to deceive us," they shouted. Soon they came with presents for the Aboona, scores of cows. But Wolff just left the animals and went on his way.

Traveling all over central Abyssinia, Wolff saw many interesting sights and preached in many towns and villages. Then he left for the coast again. On his way into the country he had visited a very strict tribe of Moslems called the Wahabites. He had left with them a number of Arabic Bibles. Later when he returned to their area, these people surrounded him angrily.

"Why did you sell us these books?" they demanded, holding up the Bibles.

"What is wrong with them?"

"They are bad books. They do not contain the name of Mohammed once."

"That," Wolff replied boldly, "should bring you to some decision."

"Yes, it has brought us to a decision," they retorted. Leaping on Wolff, they threw him to the ground and flogged him with a long whip. Then they took every penny he had, and left him so weak he could hardly stand. But he managed to limp along to another village. There some Christians put oil on his wounds and supplied him with enough money for food until he could reach the coast.

Wolff had never forgotten the wonderful weeks he had spent in India, and he desired to revisit that country. So he sailed for Bombay. Again the people welcomed him. Because it was the most unhealthful time of the year, poor Wolff was soon prostrated with a fever. He discovered that he could endure cold much better than heat. The doctors told him that if he wanted to live and work he must find a cooler country. Since he had never visited America, he decided to go there.

He sailed on a Swedish ship bound for New York. A stop was made at St. Helena, far out in the Atlantic Ocean. The governor of the island heard that Wolff was on board. He knew about the famous missionary and his adventures. He had a big gun fired, and a proclamation was made that the famous traveler Joseph Wolff was going to speak. So many people came together that they couldn't get into the church. After Wolff had preached to them in the market place, he enjoyed a pleasant visit with the governor. Landing in New York in 1837, he went about everywhere preaching. Can you imagine what he preached about? As always, his theme was the soon coming of Jesus. At that very time William Miller and his friends were preaching in New York and else where that Christ was coming soon.

There was one thing, however, that now began to trouble him. He had never been ordained as a minister of the Church of England. In New Jersey he requested ordination from the elders of the church. They agreed, and after his ordination he was assigned to be pastor of a church in Salem, Massachusetts. Wolff knew, though, that he would not stay in America long, for his family awaited him in England.

Before leaving America he had a thrilling experience. He was invited to visit Washington, where Congress was in session. One day John Quincy Adams, who had been President of the United States a few years before, stood up in Congress and moved that Joseph Wolff be invited to speak to both houses of Congress in joint session.

A short time after the motion had been carried, Wolff had the privilege of speaking to the lawmakers of America. Even President Van Buren and the Justices of the Supreme Court came to listen to him. He later told his friends that this experience was one of the greatest in his whole life.

In 1838 the restless missionary sailed away to his own country. His ever kind, always patient Georgiana welcomed him home again. She could hardly believe it when he told her that his wandering days were over, and that now he was ready to accept a pastorate of a church in England.

Upon application, he was assigned to a small parish. There Joseph and Georgiana settled down and spent several happy years together. Georgiana began to hope that perhaps her husband's restless days of wandering were really over at last.

Then one day he brought home a newspaper. It

told of how two Englishmen had gone from India to Afghanistan, and finally to Bokhara, but that nothing had been heard from them since.

Several years before, Wolff had met these two men in India and they had helped him. He feared that something dreadful had happened to them, for he knew they were daring men, who perhaps had offended the fierce rulers of Bokhara, that Moslem city.

Wolff always felt that he owed a debt to anyone who had aided him on his travels. The more he thought about it the stronger he felt that it was his duty to go and see if he could find these two men. They might be still alive, perhaps suffering in some lonely dungeon.

When he brought up the subject to Georgiana, she knew it was useless trying to stop him. So with her consent, he resigned his parish and went to see Lord Aberdeen, the leader of the government in London.

This man had heard of Wolff, and was curious to know what his next project might be. Wolff told him about his desire to find the two Englishmen and of their danger.

"Just what do you propose to do?" he asked.

"I shall go to Bokhara and find out about them."

"Do you expect to go as a representative of the British Government?"

"No, not exactly. I plan to wear the dress of the Church of England. I will carry an English and a Hebrew Bible, and I will call myself the Grand Dervish of England, Scotland, Ireland, and the whole of America. I shall demand that they give me those two men, dead or alive!"

Lord Aberdeen burst out laughing.

"You may go. But remember, we can take no responsibility for your safety. If you get caught over there, it will be beyond our power to help you. Personally, I am sure that both the men are dead."

"That may be so," Wolff replied. "But let us at least find out."

Lord Aberdeen thereupon gave Wolff a letter to the sultan of Turkey, requesting protection for him in his travels through Moslem countries.

At Constantinople he was kindly received. He even managed to preach four times in that famous city. The ambassador's wife sewed letters inside his coat, and showed him also how to hide his money. Then she made warm flannel clothing for him to wear under his Church of England attire.

The sultan sat up half the night writing letters to the various rulers of countries Wolff would pass through. Just before he left, the Russian ambassador told him that the czar had also written to many of the cities to which he would come, particularly in Persia, telling them to take good care of his friend Wolff.

Armed with these many letters, Wolff left by sea for Tabriz, whence he planned to start his overland journey to Bokhara. It had been fourteen years since he last made that trip. He shivered a bit as he recalled the time he had been stripped and beaten by robbers, and how they had talked of selling him into slavery. He wondered whether he would have any better treatment this time. Strong in faith and relying on the God of his fathers, he boldly set forth on this long, dangerous journey.

12
Face to Face
With Death

IT WAS winter when Wolff set out for Bokhara, far over the mountains and valleys of Asia.

Each day he had to wade through deep snow and face a wind so bitterly cold that it felt as though icy knives were cutting through him, in spite of the warm clothing he was wearing.

Wolff had a servant with him, but once again he had picked up a complete scoundrel. At one small town this villain, very drunk, became angry with his master, knocked him down, and proceeded to kick him. Some men in the house rushed up and knocked the servant down. When the servant became sober, Wolff spoke to him about his evil ways.

"Will you stop drinking?" the missionary asked.

"Sure I will stop," the servant replied, grinning.

Wolff had a feeling that he was being tricked.

"For how long will you stop?"

"Until I can find some more liquor!"

At that Wolff dismissed him.

At Teheran, the capital of Persia, Wolff talked with some travelers who had recently arrived from Bokhara.

"There's no question about it, Wolff," they said, "those two men you are looking for are dead."

"Then what shall I do?" Joseph muttered, more to himself than to anyone else.

"Just go straight back to England. It would be useless for you to travel hundreds of miles to help two dead men."

"No, I can't do that. People will think I am either a braggart or a humbug."

"Do you mean to say you will go to Bokhara?"

"Yes. Perhaps I can learn why they were slain and how they died."

Before leaving Teheran, Wolff visited the shah of Persia and was given letters introducing him to the ruler of Bokhara.

Again his friends urged him not to go, but he snapped his fingers and exclaimed, "I am determined to continue."

So the restless missionary traveled again, retracing the route he had followed fourteen years before. At Sebzewar, as he rode through the market place, someone recognized him. Soon crowds of people were flocking around.

"People of Mohammed," someone shouted, "wonder of wonders, signs of the times! Joseph Wolff, the English dervish, has arrived, two hundred years old!"

"No," Wolff said, "not two hundred, only forty-five!"

"No, two hundred at least. You should not be ashamed of your age. Look at your white hair!"

At Merv, Joseph heard definitely that the two Englishmen had been put to death. Again he was urged to go back, but he only shook his head. At Karakol the people who remembered him flocked around.

"You will be killed at Bokhara," they warned. When Wolff's servants heard this, they fled, and he had to go on alone.

At a small town thirty miles from Bokhara, the governor warned him.

"When you get near Bokhara you will see soldiers coming toward you with baskets. One will contain knives with which to cut you in pieces, the other will be for carrying those pieces of you back to the city!"

Undaunted, Wolff went on. As he met travelers coming from Bokhara, he heard them mutter, "There goes another victim." Surmounting the last pass, he gazed down upon Bokhara, still several miles away, and he wondered what his reception might be. Suddenly he saw a horseman emerge from the city gate and begin to come toward him. That man was carrying two baskets on his horse! Wolff shuddered and looked around for help, but he was alone.

The horseman galloped over the plain, right up to Wolff. Then to Wolff's intense relief, he saw that the man was smiling. He rook down the two baskets. One was filled with delicious fruit for Wolff to eat, and the other contained baked goods. Joseph enjoyed a feast, the first good food he had eaten in many days.

The two men went on together. Entering the gate of Bokhara once more, Wolff was surprised to find thousands of people lining the streets shouting a welcome to him.

To his intense relief, Wolff saw that the man was smiling.

In Teheran he had been carefully instructed on how to greet the emir, the ruler of the city. He was told that the two Englishmen had refused to be bothered with what they considered trifles. But Joseph listened intently.

When the hour came for him to present himself at court, he remembered all he had been told. Standing before the emir, stroking his long beard, he repeated thirty times, "Asylum of the world! Peace to the king!"

Finally the emir laughed. "Enough, enough. Come upstairs, and I will look at you."

Wolff then mounted the grand staircase and entered another audience chamber. He waited politely and patiently while the emir sat and scrutinized him. Finally he heard the king shout. "Thou strange man! Thou art a star without a tail! Neither like a Jew nor like a Hindu, nor like a Russian, thou art Joseph Wolff. Why have you come?"

"I have come seeking information about two Englishmen, Stoddard and Conolly, who came to your city two years ago and have not returned to their own country."

The emir's face grew dark with rage.

"I put them to death. They insulted me."

Changing the subject, the ruler fingered Wolff's clothing. He was still dressed like a priest of the Church of England.

"What do you mean by this kind of garment?"

"The black means I am mourning the death of my country men. The red means I am ready to shed my blood for my faith."

"I suppose you know it is a very dangerous thing for you, a Christian, to come to this city?"

Wolff nodded his head.

"There are many persons here who want me to put you to death," continued the emir. "The chief of my army, Abdul Samut Khan, says you shall not leave Bokhara alive."

Abdul Samut Khan! A vivid picture arose in Wolff's mind, for Abdul Samut Khan was the man he had pushed down the stairs many years before. He could not forget how the evil-looking man lay at the foot of the stairs muttering curses on Wolff. Now the man was in a position to fulfill his worst threats. As captain of the emir's army, it was in his power to do with Wolff whatever he pleased. The situation looked black for Wolff.

Hastily Wolff brought out all the letters he carried, demanding boldly that he be protected. After glancing through them, the ruler said, "You will be taken care of here." Clapping his hands, he bade Abdul Samut Khan enter the room!

With a look of hatred the officer walked in, his baleful glare fastened on Wolff standing before the emir.

"Take this man to his assigned quarters," the ruler commanded. Wolff was quickly led away to another part of the palace and thrust into a very plain room. He heard the key tum in the lock and knew that he was a prisoner.

Visitors were allowed him, and it was not long before he learned that the two Englishmen had indeed been killed by Abdul Samut Khan.

"Wolff," the visitors told him, "you will never leave Bokhara alive unless you become a Moslem."

"That I can never do," declared Wolff emphatically. "Never!"

The days stretched into weeks. Still Wolff was kept prisoner in the emir's palace. Often the Persian ambassador came to visit him. The shah of Persia had written three times demanding Wolff's release, but nothing had been done about it. The ambassador be came so worried lest someone come in the night and murder Wolff that he assigned one of his servants to sleep in the same room with him.

Wolff became angry when he was kept locked in that room for so long, and one day he boldly demanded to be taken to see Abdul Samut Khan. Reluctantly the guard agreed and led him into the captain's room.

"I want to leave Bokhara," Wolff stated, "and I believe you are preventing my going."

"That is absolutely true," the captain sneered.

Wolff looked steadily at that evil man, on whose face were etched the marks of lifelong cruelty. Pointing his finger at him he spoke slowly and deliberately.

"You killed Stoddard and Conolly."

Springing to his feet, the man shouted, "That's right, and I am going to kill you too! I shall repay you for what you did to me at Peshawar."

Wolff was led back to his room, sure now that he would never leave Bokhara alive.

An old Moslem teacher frequently came to reason with the Christian captive. He declared that Wolff could save his life only by accepting Mohammedanism.

"You must do it," the old man begged. "Only say once, 'God is great, and Mohammed is his prophet.' Then they will release you, and when you get back to England you can forget all about it."

"No, I can never say that," Wolff replied. "All I can say is, 'God is great, and Jesus is His divine Son.'"

The teacher left, sadly saying, "I fear I shall never see you alive again."

A few days later the public executioner came striding into Wolff's room, carrying a great sword Pointing it at Wolff's heart, he grinned and stammered, "Soon, soon!"

Wolff fully expected to be executed. Worse than even the execution might be the torture that often preceded death in those savage countries. To help him endure this, Wolff carried with him a little package of a powerful painkiller that he intended to swallow at the right time. But as he came close to death, he threw it away, and placed his whole dependence for the future upon Jesus, his Redeemer. Kneeling by the barred window, he prayed for himself and for his family so far away.

Walking over to the low table by his bed, he picked up his Bible. Opening it to one of the flyleaves he wrote a last message. "My dearest Georgiana. I have loved you unto death. Bokhara, 1844."

Then, by prayer and meditation, he fortified himself for what might come to him that day.

But on that very day a fourth and very strong letter came to the emir from the shah of Persia, and it demanded Wolff's immediate release. Being afraid to offend so powerful a ruler, the emir sent for the Persian ambassador and handed him the letter. When the ambassador had read it, the emir said, "I make you a present of the man, Joseph Wolff. He may go with you."

Immediately the prisoner was brought into the courtroom. The king spoke to him.

"Wolff, I want you to depart as a friend. Here are some presents, and here is a man who will travel with you." Then, at Wolff's feet were laid beautiful garments glittering with jewels.

"Who is this man? and where is he to go?" Wolff asked, unable as yet to grasp the full meaning of the words he had heard.

"I want him to go with you to the court of the great queen of England. I want him to be my ambassador there!"

Wolff wisely said nothing in reply. The next day he walked out of the palace a free man. He was almost overwhelmed with the sudden change in his fortunes. He had one desire, and that was to leave Bokhara as quickly as possible. As he rode his horse down the street the inhabitants of the city again turned out to cheer him, for they greatly admired the little man. In spite of this, Wolff 's only feeling was one of relief when he left the city gates behind him. This time, he knew, he was leaving Bokhara for good.

At Teheran he spoke to his companion, the man the emir wanted to send to England.

"If you are wise," he advised, "you will return to your own country. Tell the emir that he must not send you just now. The queen of England will not welcome any ambassador from a country that cruelly murders her subjects."

At this, the man turned his camel around and rode back to Bokhara.

Wolff retraced his long journey through Constantinople to England. It is interesting to note that it was in October, 1844, that he returned for the last time to England, ending his constant travels to distant lands where he had done so much to spread the wonderful message of Jesus' return.

Joseph went with Georgiana to be pastor of another parish.

There he worked faithfully for eighteen years, when God gave His restless missionary rest at last. He sleeps now. But what new travels await him—to the stars, and beyond—on the resurrection morning!

We invite you to view the complete
selection of titles we publish at:

www.TEACHServices.com

Please write or email us your praises, reactions, or
thoughts about this or any other book we publish at:

TEACH Services, Inc.
P U B L I S H I N G
www.TEACHServices.com • (800) 367-1844

P.O. Box 954
Ringgold, GA 30736

info@TEACHServices.com

TEACH Services, Inc., titles may be purchased in bulk
for educational, business, fund-raising, or sales promo-
tional use. For information, please e-mail:

BulkSales@TEACHServices.com

Finally, if you are interested in seeing
your own book in print, please contact us at

publishing@TEACHServices.com

We would be happy to review your manuscript for free.

www.ingramcontent.com/pod-product-compliance
Lightning Source LLC
Chambersburg PA
CBHW070052120426
42742CB00048B/2502